NATHALIE DUPREE COOKS QUICK MEALS FOR BUSY DAYS

ALSO BY NATHALIE DUPREE

Cooking of the South

New Southern Cooking

Nathalie Dupree's Matters of Taste

*Nathalie Dupree Cooks for
Family and Friends*

Nathalie Dupree's Southern Memories

Nathalie Dupree Cooks Great Meals for Busy Days

*Nathalie Dupree Cooks Everyday Meals
from a Well-Stocked Pantry*

NATHALIE DUPREE COOKS
QUICK MEALS
FOR BUSY DAYS

CLARKSON POTTER/PUBLISHERS

NEW YORK

THIS BOOK IS DEDICATED TO MY DEAR HUSBAND,
JACK BASS, WITH GRATITUDE FOR THE LOVE AND
SUPPORT HE HAS SHOWN.

Published by Clarkson N. Potter Inc., 201 East 50th Street, New York,
New York 10022. Member of the Crown Publishing Group.

Random House, Inc. New York, Toronto, London, Sydney, Auckland

CLARKSON N. POTTER, POTTER, and colophon are trademarks of
Clarkson N. Potter, Inc.

Manufactured in the United States of America

Design by Elizabeth Van Itallie

Library of Congress Cataloging-in-Publication Data is available upon request.

ISBN 0-517-59736-5
10 9 8 7 6 5 4 3 2 1
First Edition

ACKNOWLEDGMENTS

Frequently I am asked where I get my recipes. They often come spontaneously, but I always try to credit anyone who gives me an idea for a recipe. Whenever I read a cookbook, I add the name to my bibliography, and if I use or adapt the recipe, I mention it in a head-note. Those individuals' names follow. Some of the following worked for me on my PBS crew, others worked for the TV Food Network, and still others helped with little kindnesses in a difficult year.

Moises Alvarez, John Baker, Jack Bass, Amanda Brown-Olmstead, Kay Calvert, Carol Cutler, Lauren Deen, Georgia Downard, Norma Driebe, David Dupree, Finnish Tourist Bureau, Derek Flynn, Pierre Franey, Cynthia Hizer, Martine Jolly, Lynne Kearney, Ursula Knaeusel, Ralph and Marjorie Knowles, Pam Krauss, James Kreiser, Carole Landon, Ric Lands, Catherine Lowe, Maureen Luchejko, Melissa Lynch, John Markham, Kelly McNabb, Beverly Molander, Gretchen Moore, Barbara Morgan, Leslie Orlandini, Ray Overton, Jackie Roberts, Lyn Saathoff, Lee Ann Saye, Wendy Schuman, Emily Schwartz, Patti Scott, Lauren Shakely, Sigal Seeber, Tina Sharpe, Susan Stockton, Ricki Stofsky, Margaret Ann Surber, Judy Tabb, Anne Tamsberg, Elizabeth Vaeth, Virginia Willis, Jody Weatherstone, Sally Young, and Dini Diskin-Zimmerman.

CONTENTS

INTRODUCTION

There are many reasons for writing a book. Since this is a book I never thought I'd write, it needs a bit of explanation by way of introduction.

Cooking has been my hobby and my joy, as well as my career, for many years. In the past I would think nothing of spending several hours in the kitchen. Cooking gives me a boost, makes the house smell inviting, and ensures that I and those around me will have something wonderful to eat. All in all, it's a good use of my time.

Then reality hit, crashingly. Getting those few hours to cook became a luxury. My elderly parents' declining health meant that I spent increasingly more time attending to their needs. I have a new marriage, and my time is not my own anymore. And my hobby-turned-business keeps me on the road many weeks of the year.

My last two books, *Great Meals for Busy Days* and *Everyday Meals from a Well-Stocked Pantry,* reflected the reality of my needs in all ways but one—getting the meal on the table in a rush. And that is the thrust of this book, the third of the trilogy. Making dinner when I spent my days juggling competing commitments became a shortcut affair.

And so I made changes in the way I approached meal planning and preparation. With grocery shopping time limited, I had to plan ahead. I kept it as short as possible, going only once a week to shop. I learned to buy as many prepared ingredients at the grocery store as possible, without resorting to "ready-made." I *did* buy jarred roasted peppers, sliced vegetables, cut-up melons, pretrimmed meat, chopped garlic, prewashed spinach, sliced wild mushroom mixtures, farm-grown mussels that need no scrubbing or debearding, and many other convenience items ready to be mixed, sautéed, or grilled and served with a minimum of fuss. By and large, I found that, during the week, I needed a meal on the table in half an hour. (I gave myself longer for special meals, weekends, and holidays.)

I used shortcuts in other areas as well. Rather than give up on making fresh yeast breads altogether, I used the microwave, or substituted nonyeast breads. It's my belief that even the busiest cook should find a moment once in a while to make his or her own bread—the activity is good for the cook's soul.

I took liberties with all the cuisines I like—Italian, Indian, Spanish, French, Mexican, Asian, and even Southern—and shortcut them, depending more heavily on prepared foods and condiments such as hoisin sauce, canned water chestnuts, chile paste, and pesto.

However, old habits die hard. I didn't stop doing as much preparation as possible in advance just because I was cooking at the last minute: I still measured ingredients early in the day so that when I rushed in I wouldn't have to wonder where the sesame seeds really were or if I had any rice wine vinegar. I tended to avoid using really exotic ingredients that would have meant a trip to ethnic markets or searching for unusual produce not available at my super-market. My beloved Parmigiano-Reggiano cheese pulled me out of many time scrapes, elevating a salad, pasta dish, or even fruit dessert to the realm of something special. Occasionally I'd indulge in something decadently expensive like fresh Portobello or shiitake mushrooms or balsamic vinegar. Such touches give a meal cachet without much effort, justifying their added expense.

Otherwise I watched my budget rather carefully. This kind of cooking is inherently more expensive because easily cooked ingredients often command a premium price. Scallopini and preboned pieces of meat that require attention from the butcher tend to cost more. In addition, these cuts don't offer the abundance of leftovers that a roast does. I tried to double the recipes whenever appropriate and freeze the leftovers in small containers that reheat quickly in the microwave or oven.

It is clear to me that preparing meals "off the cuff" is not the way I want to cook forever. This frantic, last-minute push—setting the table, chopping, slicing, and stir-frying—is not geared toward gracious living. It does, however, enable me to fix dinner for my husband and family—a joy to me. I know what I am eating, rather than relying on something commercially prepared, and the food tastes better. As a bonus, my house smells good and my family feels my love that way as well.

There are some basic rules for quick cooking. The smaller (and thinner) something is—whether a potato or pork chop—the quicker it will cook. This aids speedy cooking for small groups. When sautéing for more than four or six, it is better to use two sauté pans, or to get thicker pieces of meat like chops instead of scallopini if you don't want to spend all your time standing over a pan. Two woks or frying pans might also be necessary if stir-frying a large quantity. For this reason, most of the sautéing recipes are meant to serve four.

Organization is the key to easy cooking. I can't imagine the trepidation with which a cook who had no idea what dinner was to be that night would approach the pantry. If this happens night after night, please heed my advice and make a menu plan for the week. It will go a long way toward reducing the stress you feel when you don't know what you are going to fix and you are hungry and tired yourself. I also recommend a "no-brainer" list for those times when the plan fails. I posted one on a door in my kitchen; it says, for instance, "clam spaghetti" and lists a few ingredients. So, when I am too hungry to think, I make spaghetti with clams. Another is "pizza, classic"—tomato sauce, cheese, herbs, pizza crust.

Another aspect of organization is to chop and slice as much as possible in advance. It is important to consider the amount of time it will take slicing and dicing as well as cooking. I chop my vegetables on the weekends, when I have more time, and store them. I wash my lettuce (if it needs it; much of what's available today doesn't!) as soon as I unload the groceries. I try to have something cooking—chicken stock, onion soup, cornish hens—or at least marinating while I unload the groceries.

Once I've settled on my menu, I decide what is to be cooked first, second, or third. Often the side dishes should be nearly done before a last-minute sauté is begun. This timing is crucial when dealing with thin pieces of meat or fish.

When you find something that works for you, repeat it. List it in the no-brainers on the side of your door—with the recipe source if necessary—and prepare it once every week or so. Somehow, we have come to value variety perhaps more than it really deserves. When I was growing up, many households repeated their menus weekly. You needn't be quite that monotonous, although children actually prefer something familiar. Throughout the book you will find lists of suggestions for whetters, quickie desserts, and the like; supplement these with your own ideas for nearly instant recipes.

Whenever possible, make twice as much as you need. Pasta, rice, and even some potato dishes fall into this category. Both pasta and rice may be reheated in boiling water or in the microwave. I'm not a fan of quick-cook rice, but I do like quick-cook couscous and find that it reheats very nicely. Like rice and pasta, it is terrific in a salad the next day, or a few days later, changing its personality completely. Freeze leftovers in small containers for quick reheating.

To help you make the best decision on how to allocate your precious resources of time, I have annotated the recipes with icons that indicate which will freeze ❄, and which can be made ahead and reheated ⚡. I've also pointed out those that can be made mostly from pantry staples 🥫 supplemented with fresh (or defrosted) meat, fruits, or vegetables, and those that are virtually one-dish meals 🍲, needing only a salad or a loaf of crusty bread to round things out, thus saving time and thought on choosing side dishes and accompaniments. And when someting a bit special is in order, choose the recipes marked 🍴 ; these are festive dishes that are still quick enough for weeknight entertaining. Virtually any recipe be speeded along by partial or total advance preparation; consider slicing vegetables, mixing up marinades and dressings, or even grilling meats or vegetables several hours (or even days in some cases) before you complete assembly of the disk. There's nearly always something you can do ahead of time, even if it's only grating citrus peel or chopping garlic or herbs. Yet all of these steps will save precious minutes when it comes time to cook. Most of all, I urge the harried cook, don't be hard on yourself. Don't criticize yourself when you open a can of soup and pour it over some vegetables. If that's the best you can do today, enjoy it! Tomorrow is another day, and perhaps then you'll have some time and energy for a little more inventiveness. I still remember my mother's bean and mushroom soup dish, and it was pretty good.

Almond Roasted Cheese ■ Mozzarella en Carozza ■ Salmon
Tartare ■ Stewed Calamari ■ Grits with Shrimp ■ Blink-of-the-Eye
Antipasto ■ Olive Sauce ■ Grilled Peanut Butter and Banana Triangles ■

WHETTERS

Cumin Sticks ■ Tomato Bruschetta ■ Lime and Herb Dip ■
Marinated Dried Tomatoes and Basil ■ Sally's Banana Salsa ■ Chunky
Tomato Salsa ■ Tomatillo Salsa ■ Grilled Eggplant Pinwheels

IN THIS ERA of frantic activity, guests are often invited to the house for drinks and a visit before going off, perhaps, to an office party or a larger gathering. It is at the last minute that plans are made about where to gather, and it is particularly nice to offer one's home with assurance that the pantry can provide some bits and pieces to set the evening off with a sparkle.

Whetters, or appetizers, are also wonderful stopgaps to getting a meal on the table. A "little something" will frequently give the harried cook a welcome breather while everything else is pulled together. These savory tidbits silence the complainer and bring a touch of graciousness to a meal.

The ideal whetter piques the appetite and lets people think they've gotten something to eat, without filling them up. In a perfect world, one could reach into the cabinet or freezer and come up with one or two things that, when combined, would be so glamorous, so exciting and yet so effortless, that the appearance of total calmness and dominion would settle over the kitchen.

These simple things used to be ritualized. There was cream cheese spread with hot pepper jelly (now called jalapeño jelly) served with saltines. Peanuts, pecans, and walnuts have been joined by cashews, and all of them, plain or roasted with seasonings, are still ever welcome.

Other stand-bys were herring and sour cream and prosciutto wrapped around melon. These simple things ought, indeed, to be remembered at times of desperation no matter where one lives. Even easier are such

QUICK IDEAS FOR WHETTERS

- Cut Parmigiano-Reggiano into bite-size pieces and drizzle with the best balsamic vinegar you can find.
- Wrap melon wedges with thin slices of prosciutto or country ham; drizzle with crème de menthe, Midori (melon liqueur), or Kirsch; or sprinkle with chopped mint.
- Drizzle small tomatoes with olive oil and toss with parsley and small imported black olives.
- Split a quail, sprinkle with butter or oil, and broil quickly. Cut into quarters and serve hot.

• Fill a baking dish with rock salt or crumpled foil. Set opened oysters and their juice in the curved half of the shell in the dish and broil for 2 to 3 minutes.
• Toss blanched asparagus or watercress in a vinaigrette with roasted or grilled red peppers, scallops, shrimp, or grilled chicken tenders.
• Wrap pecan halves or walnut halves with small pieces of thinly sliced prosciutto.
• Slice an onion and sauté in butter until golden brown. Add balsamic vinegar, salt, and pepper and serve on toast or pita points.

stalwarts as chips and dip, crackers and a cheese ball you've stashed in the freezer for just such an occasion, Italian olives and French cornichons, saltines and kippers, sliced tomatoes and mozzarella with basil—all virtually instant hors d'oeuvres.

To update this repertoire, serve some Parmigiano-Reggiano drizzled with balsamic vinegar and a colorfully arrayed antipasto of red peppers, artichokes, and other Italian delicacies, a fresher take on the crudités of the 60s.

Something baked—whether a simple bruschetta or cumin–laden pastries—gives the appearance of preplanning and organization even when taking less time to make than many other baked goods. Ideally, the pastries are in the freezer. If not, they may still be made at the last minute and are simple enough that they can be pulled out within minutes of opening the front door to the first arrivals.

Sometimes, if the array of whetters is beautiful and the conversation engrossing, whetters can become meals in themselves— requiring perhaps just the addition of a salad to round things out. If you happen to have gone ahead and fixed a main course anyway—save it for another day!

ALMOND ROASTED CHEESE

I find a bit of soft cheese and French bread will hold off hunger pangs while I prepare the rest of the meal. This perky cheese log freezes well, tightly wrapped, so make an extra to have on hand. (Reheat in the microwave for 15 to 20 seconds.) I sometimes offer Granny Smith apple wedges in place of the bread.

¼ cup finely chopped blanched almonds
¼ cup dry breadcrumbs

1 8-ounce package Neufchâtel or cream cheese
1 loaf French bread, sliced

Preheat the oven to 400° F. Grease a baking sheet with nonstick spray. Combine the almonds and breadcrumbs on a plate or baking sheet. Cut the cheese in half lengthwise. Roll each half in the nut–crumb mixture, pressing the nut-crumb mixture into the cheese and elongating the cheese into a log 1½ inches in diameter and 8 inches long. Place both logs on the prepared baking sheet and bake until the crust is crisp and the cheese is warmed, 5 to 10 minutes.

Serves 6 to 8

Variation: Blend chopped herbs into the cheese in the food processor, then bread and shape into a log as above.

BREADCRUMBS IN A JIFFY
Making your own breadcrumbs is economical and allows you to blend whole wheat, pumpernickel, or egg breads with white bread for different flavors. For best results, allow the breads to dry out thoroughly in a paper bag (plastic may cause molding) before pulverizing in a food processor. You can accumulate odds and ends in the freezer to make custom blends at a moment's notice; no need to thaw before grinding the bread.

Mozzarella en Carozza

Ithink of this as a heavenly melted cheese French toast, yet that doesn't quite do it justice. Pair this wonderful appetizer with a substantial Italian minestrone for a complete meal. The sandwiches are served hot, and the cheese melts in your mouth.

3 ¼-inch-thick slices mozzarella
6 slices white bread, crusts removed
1 cup all-purpose flour
2 large eggs

1 teaspoon salt
½ teaspoon pepper
1 cup dry breadcrumbs
½ cup vegetable oil

Place the mozzarella between the slices of bread to form 3 sandwiches. Cut each sandwich to form 12 triangles.

Place the flour in a pie tin or plate. Whisk together the eggs, salt, and pepper, and place in a second pie plate. Place the breadcrumbs in a third pie plate. Dip the triangles in the flour, then in the seasoned egg, and finally in the breadcrumbs. At this point, the triangles may be refrigerated for up to 8 hours or frozen for 3 months.

Heat the oil in a large, deep skillet to 350°F. Fry the triangles until light golden brown, about 4 minutes, turning if necessary. Serve hot.

Serves 3 to 6

SALMON TARTARE

There are endless ways to serve uncooked chopped salmon; it accommodates itself to all sorts of flavors—soy sauce and ginger, cilantro and chiles, curry and onions. This version is a takeoff on the classic beef tartare, sans the traditional egg. For this and any uncooked salmon recipe, it is imperative to use farm-raised salmon because their diets are controlled, reducing the likelihood of parasites. Serve this simple and elegant appetizer surrounded by cucumber slices and accompanied with a tangy topping.

1 8-ounce salmon fillet, skinned, or 1 cup salmon trimmings and scraps (see sidebar)
3 tablespoons shallots, finely chopped
1 tablespoon capers, finely chopped
Salt
White pepper
1 seedless cucumber, peeled and thinly sliced
1 cup sour cream or Lime and Herb Dip (page 27)

Finely chop the salmon. Place in a small bowl and stir in the shallots and capers. Season to taste with salt and pepper. When ready to serve, place a small amount on a plate and surround with cucumber slices. Place a dollop of sour cream or dip on top.

Serves 6 to 8

Note: To prepare in the food processor, first slice the cucumbers and remove. Next chop the shallots, then the capers, removing each when done. Then carefully chop the salmon. It is best to have the salmon nearly frozen when chopping in the food processor.

Stewed Calamari

CLEANING SQUID

Readying squid for cooking is not difficult, but it can be time-consuming. Since squid is so economical to begin with, buying it already cleaned is certainly worth the small additional cost when time is tight.

To do it yourself, first remove the head from the body. Inside the head is the beak; this needs to be removed. Sever the head from the tentacles; reserve the tentacles. Remove the clear, bonelike piece from the interior of the squid body. Thoroughly wash the tentacles and body. Peel the outer layer of skin off the body. This comes off very easily under cold running water. Cut the body into ⅛- to ¼-inch rings.

Squid (calamari) is very inexpensive and versatile and makes for an unusual and unexpected starter. If you can't find squid, substitute an equal amount of cleaned shrimp. This Italian-inspired dish is called a stew but actually cooks in just minutes especially if you start with cleaned squid. It's wonderful served with crusty bread to sop up the delicious sauce. Don't hesitate to use up the stems of the parsley and rosemary that you have used elsewhere in this dish—the stems are very flavorful and should not be wasted or thrown away. Save them for soup stock, too.

1 tablespoon olive oil	BOUQUET GARNI
1 medium onion, chopped	2 parsley stems
1 garlic clove, peeled and finely chopped	2 rosemary stems
1 20-ounce can whole tomatoes,	6 to 8 peppercorns
broken up	3 tablespoons chopped parsley
	1 pound cleaned squid (see sidebar)
	Salt
	Freshly ground black pepper

Heat the olive oil on low heat in a heavy 2-quart saucepan. Add the onion and cook until soft and translucent, about 3 minutes. Add the garlic, tomatoes, and the bouquet garni tied in a cheesecloth. Bring to the boil, reduce the heat, and simmer for about 10 minutes.

Add the squid rings and tentacles or shrimp to the simmering sauce. Cook 2 to 3 minutes until white, then remove from the heat immediately; the squid will be rubbery if it is overcooked. Season to taste with salt and pepper, remove the bouquet garni, and serve immediately.

Serves 4 to 6

GRITS WITH SHRIMP

Long served in Charleston, this appetizer, with many variations, is very popular not just all over the South, but in trendy restaurants from New York to Seattle. I confess I do use it as a main course for brunch as well. It reheats well in the microwave, and I have kept it in a low oven for a long time in a casserole dish with good results. The shrimp may be precooked at the grocery store or sautéed fresh.

3 cups milk

1 cup half-and-half

1 cup quick grits

6 tablespoons butter

3 cloves garlic, peeled and chopped

1 medium onion, chopped

1 to 1½ cups blue cheese

2 to 3 tablespoons Worcestershire sauce

Hot sauce to taste

Salt

Freshly ground black pepper

½ pound medium peeled shrimp, cooked
   or uncooked

Combine the milk and half-and-half in a heavy nonstick saucepan and heat nearly to the boil. Stir in the grits and cook 5 to 10 minutes, stirring occasionally to prevent burning. Heat 3 tablespoons of the butter in a heavy frying pan. Add the garlic and the onion and cook until soft, about 5 to 8 minutes. Stir the garlic, onions, and butter into the grits. Season to taste with the cheese, Worcestershire, hot sauce, salt, and pepper. Melt the remaining 3 tablespoons butter, and sauté the shrimp just until cooked through, about 2 minutes on each side. Pour the butter and shrimp into the grits, stirring to combine. Leave a good splash of shrimp on top.

Serves 4 to 6

BLINK-OF-THE-EYE ANTIPASTO

I have an Italian friend, known for her great cooking, who can have a dazzling antipasto ready in the blink of an eye. Red peppers, artichoke hearts, and meats and cheeses gleaned from the deli or supermarket, bathed in herbs and oil, glimmer from the buffet. Her secret? This is one occasion when using ingredients from jars is nearly as good as serving laboriously obtained fresh ones and is certainly a blessed relief from the pressure of time. Do not throw away the liquid from the jars in case you don't use up all the ingredients. If there are no leftovers, the juices themselves are flavorful and can add zest to dressings and other dishes. If you are grilling or broiling the onions, brush them with oil and cook for 6 to 8 minutes before you begin to assemble the antipasto.

1 12-ounce jar roasted bell peppers, whole or sliced

1 6-ounce jar marinated artichoke hearts

2 to 4 ounces good-quality anchovies or sardines

6 ounces peperoncini or other pickled peppers

¼ cup imported green or black olives, preferably Italian or French

2 tablespoons olive oil (optional)

2 garlic cloves, peeled and chopped

¼ cup red wine vinegar

1 to 2 tablespoons chopped fresh oregano (optional)

1 to 2 tablespoons chopped fresh basil (optional)

½ cup grated imported Parmesan cheese

2 onions, quartered and grilled or roasted (optional)

Place the peppers on a medium-size platter. Remove the artichoke hearts from the jar, and taste the marinade. If it is flavorful, place the marinade in a bowl. Arrange the artichoke hearts next to the peppers. Arrange the anchovies or sardines on the platter and drizzle with the oil from their can or discard, depending on your preference. Arrange the peperoncini and olives on the plate. Mix together the oil or artichoke marinade and garlic. Add the red wine vinegar. Sprinkle the vegetables with the mixture, then the fresh herbs if using, and the Parmesan. Garnish with the grilled onions, if desired.

Serves 4 to 6

Olive Sauce

This is spectacular for spreading on toast or pita bread points or pouring over meats and pastas. Use it in place of butter. Pitting olives takes time; they are now available prepitted in upscale grocery stores.

1/3 cup olive oil

1 1/2 cups Greek, French, or Italian black olives, pitted and drained

3 shallots, peeled and finely chopped

2 garlic cloves, peeled and finely chopped

2 tablespoons fresh herbs, preferably rosemary, marjoram, and parsley, finely chopped

1/2 cup red wine vinegar

Heat 2 tablespoons of the oil in a saucepan. Meanwhile, chop the olives in a food processor. Add the olives, shallots, and garlic to the saucepan and cook until soft. Add the chopped herbs, the rest of the olive oil, and the vinegar. Bring to the boil and cook down until you have 1 cup.

Makes 1 cup

PITA CRISPS
These homemade "crackers" are a snap to make and a lowfat treat to boot. To make them, split the pitas and cut each half into eighths. Arrange on a baking sheet. If desired, brush the triangles lightly with melted butter or oil. Bake in a 400° F. oven or toaster oven, or broil quickly until lightly browned. These crisps are particularly good with hummus and other store-bought dips and spreads—perfect for last-minute company. Make a large batch and store them in an airtight container for up to 2 weeks.

Grilled Peanut Butter and Banana Triangles

My husband will not be winning a cooking award any time soon, but he does have one specialty, which he first served me when we were courting. He learned it at Elvis Presley's hangout in Memphis and, as a joke, started serving it to friends, who would scarf it up. It is certainly a conversation piece, and surprisingly pleasing. Perhaps it's comfort food for adults who would not admit to needing such a thing.

4 slices Italian, French, or sourdough bread

1/3 cup peanut butter

1 large banana

3 tablespoons butter

Spread 2 slices of the bread with the peanut butter. Slice the banana thickly and place on the peanut butter. Top with the remaining bread. Heat the butter in a nonstick frying pan or electric grill. Add the sandwiches and fry on one side until toasted, turn, and toast second side. (Alternately, cook on an electric grill until both sides are toasted.) Cut each sandwich into 4 triangles and serve hot.

Makes 8 pieces

CUMIN STICKS

Ouzo, a Greek liquor with a strong licorice flavor, is the traditional flavoring for these addictive little tidbits. However, I prefer to use ground fennel seeds instead. This recipe is adapted from one in *The Complete Book of Greek Cooking,* by the Recipe Club of St. Paul's Greek Orthodox Cathedral. Kefalotiri is a sharp, strong cheese that can be replaced with a sharp white cheddar or Romano. The food processor makes this very fast; grate the cheese first, then make the dough in the same bowl. Rolling the dough between sheets of wax paper reduces cleanup time.

2 cups all-purpose flour
1 teaspoon salt
½ teaspoon dry mustard
1 teaspoon ground fennel seeds
½ cup grated Kefalotiri cheese
1 cup (2 sticks) butter, melted

1 egg yolk
6 tablespoons water
1 egg white, lightly beaten
1 teaspoon cumin seeds
½ teaspoon fennel seeds

Preheat the oven to 375°F. Grease a cookie sheet.

In a food processor or bowl, mix together the flour, salt, mustard, ground fennel seeds, and cheese. Add the butter, egg yolk, and water to form a soft dough. Roll out the dough between pieces of wax paper to ¼-inch thickness. Cut into 3 × ½-inch strips with a pizza or pastry cutter. Place on the cookie sheet. Brush with the egg white and sprinkle with the cumin and fennel seeds. Bake until light brown, about 15 minutes. Serve warm or at room temperature.

Makes 4 dozen

TOMATO BRUSCHETTA

A trip to Tuscany, where I was served innumerable variations of toasted bread with a savory, flavorful topping, showed me how many ways the treat known as bruschetta can be enhanced. At its simplest, ripe Romas are tossed with oil and basil and placed on garlic-rubbed, toasted bread, for a flavor that is balanced among sweet, sour, bitter, and salty characteristics. This version offers the option of some embellishments, such as chopped anchovies or balsamic vinegar, but even without these additions it's a most appealing appetite whetter.

8 Roma tomatoes, cored, seeded, and
   chopped
2 tablespoons extra-virgin olive oil
1 tablespoon chopped fresh basil
½ cup chopped onion (optional)
¼ cup capers, chopped (optional)
1 tablespoon chopped fresh parsley
   (optional)

1 tablespoon red wine or balsamic
   vinegar (optional)
8 anchovy fillets, finely chopped
   (optional)
Salt
Freshly ground black pepper
6 thick slices Italian bread, toasted
1 garlic clove, peeled

Combine the tomatoes, olive oil, and basil, plus as many of the optional ingredients as you choose, in a bowl. Season to taste with salt and pepper. Set aside. Rub the toasted bread with the garlic. Top with the tomato mixture and serve immediately.

Serves 4 to 6

Variation: Sauté 1 chopped onion in 2 tablespoons of olive oil until brown, about 4 minutes. Add ½ pound quartered chicken livers and cook 3 to 5 minutes. Stir in 2 tablespoons balsamic vinegar and simmer 2 to 3 minutes. Spoon this mixture onto the garlic toast in place of the tomatoes.

LIME AND HERB DIP

PRECOOKING ARTICHOKES

Artichokes require a rather long cooking period, making them a poor choice for last-minute meals. However, steamed or microwaved artichokes store well. So make twice as many as you need and serve some hot the first day, and the rest a day or two later, filled with a flavored mayonnaise or yogurt dip for a next-to-instant appetizer. Steam trimmed artichokes in a scant inch of boiling water for 30 to 45 minutes; invert on paper towels to drain, then wrap tightly and refrigerate up to 2 days.

Here is a lean alternative to mayonnaise-based dips and dressings. I like citrusy sauces as a condiment for boiled artichokes; pull out the inner leaves, scoop out the choke with a teaspoon, and ladle in some of the dip.

½ cup finely chopped fresh parsley
½ cup finely chopped fresh cilantro leaves
Finely chopped peel (no white attached) of 1 lime
Juice of 2 limes
Finely chopped peel (no white attached) of 1 lemon
Juice of 2 lemons
1 cup lowfat plain yogurt
Salt
Freshly ground black pepper

Combine the parsley, cilantro, lime peel, lime juice, lemon peel, lemon juice, and yogurt in a bowl. Season well with salt and pepper. Chill until ready to serve. May be made ahead and refrigerated for several days.

Makes 2 cups

MARINATED DRIED TOMATOES AND BASIL

DRIED TOMATOES

If you can't seem to keep enough fresh tomatoes on hand, try having a stash of sun-dried tomatoes in the pantry. They have a distinctive flavor and are nice with a variety of pastas and main dishes. Dried tomatoes come dry or packed in oil. The oil-packed are usually more expensive, but are better for quick-cooking because they're ready to use; soaking the dry variety usually adds 10 to 15 minutes to a recipe.

I use these tomatoes and the luscious oil they are packed in on pizza, with pasta, on top of goat cheese—any number of ways. Use the more economical dry, unreconstituted tomatoes for this recipe.

12 sun-dried tomatoes (packed in oil)
1 cup whole fresh basil leaves
2 garlic cloves, peeled and chopped
1 cup extra-virgin olive oil

Layer the tomatoes, basil, and garlic in a sterilized 1-pint jar. The tomatoes may be used whole, sliced, or chopped. Add enough of the oil to cover completely and close the jar tightly. Refrigerate at least a week and up to 3 months. Add oil as needed to keep the ingredients covered as you use the tomatoes.

Makes 1 pint

SALLY'S BANANA SALSA

Even if you chop the other ingredients in a food processor, chop the bananas by hand and stir them in last. This salsa tastes best when served 2 to 3 hours after making.

2 large bananas, peeled and chopped
    into ¼-inch pieces
1 red bell pepper, seeded and chopped
    into ¼-inch pieces
1 green bell pepper, seeded and chopped
    into ¼-inch pieces
1 or 2 jalapeño peppers, finely chopped
3 green onions, finely chopped

1 tablespoon chopped fresh ginger
3 tablespoons fresh lime or lemon juice
¼ cup chopped fresh mint leaves
¼ teaspoon ground cardamom
2 tablespoons packed light brown sugar
Salt
Freshly ground black pepper

Combine the bananas, red bell pepper, green bell pepper, jalapeño peppers, green onions, ginger, lime or lemon juice, mint, cardamom, and brown sugar in a bowl and gently toss to mix. Season to taste with salt and pepper. Refrigerate, covered, until ready to serve.

Makes 3 cups

CHUNKY TOMATO SALSA

Salsa has rapidly overtaken ketchup as the condiment of choice. This is a terrific recipe, easily thrown together with a few fresh ingredients and pantry staples. Canned tomatoes with Mexican herbs really simplify preparation.

1 14½-ounce can salsa-style chunky
    tomatoes
2 garlic cloves, peeled and finely chopped
Juice of 2 lemons
3 green onions, sliced ⅛-inch thick
1 tablespoon olive oil

2 tablespoons chopped fresh parsley
1 avocado, pitted, peeled, and cut into
    ½-inch pieces
Salt
Freshly ground black pepper

**SALSA IN
A SNAP**
Almost anything can be chopped fairly fine, blended with acid of some kind and a few fresh herbs, and be called a salsa. Many fruits are wonderful salsa additions, especially tropical fruits, fresh or canned, such as pineapple, mango, papaya, as well as avocados and tomatoes. Be sure to have a variety of textures: Add jicama, bell pepper, or onion for crunch, tomato or cucumber for a softer texture. Just use whatever you have in the vegetable drawer or pantry, add a splash of olive oil and citrus juice or vinegar, stir in fresh, preserved, or even dried herbs, and let sit for 30 minutes or so to blend the flavors. If it's chunky enough, salsa can act as a saladlike side dish to grilled fish or meat.

In a medium mixing bowl, combine the tomatoes, garlic, lemon juice, green onions, oil, parsley, and avocado. Stir well to combine. Season to taste with salt and pepper.

Makes 2½ cups

TOMATILLO SALSA

The slightly astringent flavor of tomatillos makes this salsa great with beef tenderloin, roast pork, or chicken, and it is an excellent dip for tortillas or a topping for cream cheese served with crackers. This does not freeze, but it will last 1 week in the refrigerator.

4 garlic cloves, peeled and chopped
1½ pounds tomatillos, husks removed and cored
2 poblano peppers, roasted, peeled, and seeded
2 4-ounce cans green chiles, drained
1 small red bell pepper, seeded and chopped
1 small red onion, chopped

2 or 3 jalapeño peppers, seeded and chopped
2 tablespoons vegetable oil (optional)
1 tablespoon red wine vinegar
Juice of 1 lime
2 tablespoons chopped fresh cilantro
1 to 2 teaspoons ground cumin
1 to 2 teaspoons chili powder
¼ to ½ teaspoon cayenne pepper
Salt
Freshly ground black pepper

Combine the garlic, tomatillos, poblano peppers, green chiles, red pepper, red onion, and jalapeño. Pour the mixture into a large colander to drain any excess liquid. Return the drained mixture to a large bowl and add the vegetable oil, if using, red wine vinegar, lime juice, cilantro, cumin, chili powder, cayenne pepper, and salt and pepper to taste. It is best refrigerated 4 hours before serving to allow the flavors to develop fully, but it can be served right away.

Makes 2½ cups

GRILLED EGGPLANT PINWHEELS

The next time you are grilling, take advantage of the hot grill. Slice and cook an eggplant to use within a day or two. When you start with precooked eggplant slices, this attractive hot appetizer is ready in about 15 minutes. If you prefer to reduce the amount of fat, use nonfat yogurt cheese (page 76) instead of goat cheese and use nonstick spray for the eggplant rather than oil.

QUICK-COOK EGGPLANT

Brushing eggplant slices with oil and grilling, baking, or broiling is actually much faster than frying them in a skillet and uses far less oil. I can always find uses for extra cooked eggplant, like a quick moussaka, vegetable frittata, focaccia, or an overstuffed sandwich with mozzarella cheese, so I frequently cook twice as much as I need for a given recipe.

1 eggplant
¼ cup oil
Salt
Freshly ground black pepper
4 ounces soft goat cheese, such as
    Montrachet

2 tablespoons chopped fresh thyme or
    oregano
1 10-ounce jar whole roasted red peppers, drained

Preheat the oven to 350°F. Grease a 9 × 12-inch baking dish.

Slice the eggplant lengthwise into ¼-inch slices. Brush lightly on both sides with oil and season with salt and pepper. Grill 3 to 5 minutes on each side until softened and lightly browned.

In a small bowl, combine the cheese and thyme until smooth. Season with salt and pepper.

To assemble, top an eggplant slice with a red pepper slice. Place 1 tablespoon of the cheese mixture on the red pepper. Starting at the smaller end, roll up into a pinwheel. Place seam-side down in the baking dish. Bake 8 to 10 minutes until heated through.

Serves 4 to 6

Variation: Add 1 leaf of wilted spinach between eggplant and red pepper for a more colorful dish.

Cold Avocado Soup ■ *Strawberry Soup* ■ *All You Need Soup* ■
Chilled Citrus-Blueberry Soup ■ *Black Bean Gazpacho* ■ *Roasted
Corn and Pepper Chowder* ■ *Fast Pantry Pasta e Fagioli* ■ *Vegetarian
Gumbo* ■ *Spinach Soup* ■ *White Bean or Lentil and Sausage Soup*
■ *Basic Vinaigrette* ■ *Tarragon Mayonnaise* ■ *Apple Waldorf Chicken Salad*
■ *Cold Salmon and Almond Salad* ■ *Lacy Green Salad* ■

SOUPS AND
SALADS

Watercress and Bacon Salad ■ *Warm Broccoli-Mushroom Salad* ■
Shredded Carrot Slaw with Poppy Seed Vinaigrette ■ *Cauliflower
with Herbed Vinaigrette* ■ *Chilled Pine Nut and Celery
Coucous Salad* ■ *Pear and Blue Cheese Salad* ■ *Green Salad
with Apples and Parmesan Vinaigrette* ■ *Oriental Salad with
Sesame Soy Vinaigrette* ■ *Vegetables in Lemon Vinaigrette*

THE WORLD OF FOOD is constantly changing and evolving. When I was classically trained in the French manner, I thought of soups as starters and salads as something served after the main course. That is certainly the way I did it in the days when I had my restaurant in the country between Social Circle and Covington, Georgia. I clung to fixed rituals of service, and the order in which parts of the meal were served was important to me. Hearty soups would have been casual fare—for lunch, maybe, or a Sunday-night supper.

All of that is old news. Now I look at a meal as a whole, considering both the time spent on preparation as well as the calories. I am happy to serve a wonderful grilled sandwich with a hearty soup for a major meal. I delight in transforming leftovers from the refrigerator into substantial, satisfying salads—in fact, that is perhaps my favorite way to devise a meal these days. Take a vinaigrette or a favorite salad dressing and combine it with what is in the refrigerator or on the pantry shelf, whether grilled chicken breast, canned beans, seafood, or vegetables. Season well, use fresh herbs when possible to punch up the flavor, and you will have a terrific main-course salad. The salad ingredients available change radically from locale to locale. There is no mesclun mix in my grocery store in Oxford, Mississippi. In Atlanta, there are many new mixes of baby lettuces and arugula, as well as mesclun. I feel free to develop my own mixes.

More and more I rely on soups to speed my meals along. Yes, I love cooking soups that simmer on the back of the stove for hours when I have the time at home. But for both hot meals and cold, soup can be made quickly with little sacrifice of flavor.

When making cold soup, use chilled ingredients as much as possible. For instance, put cans of black beans and tomato juice for Black Bean Gazpacho in the refrigerator early in the day—or even store some there if you make it regularly. If the soup requires chilling, use the freezer to speed the process.

For hot soups, cook twice as much onions, other vegetables, and pasta as you need and refrigerate half. Use the second half to start your soup another day. Use canned peas and beans rather than dried ones, rinsing if necessary, to eliminate soaking time.

It should go without saying that you should save all vegetable cooking liquids. They enhance soups enormously, both in nutrition and in flavor. If you have time, boil them down to reduce the liquid; they'll take less room in the refrigerator. When chicken or beef stock is called for, use some of the vegetable liquid and add a bouillon cube.

I combine hot and cold, serving cold salad with hot meat, cold soup with a hot sandwich, or a hot soup with a cold salad, in ways that please my palate and my craving for texture and color.

In this chapter, soups and salads are mixed with abandon. You are not locked in to using them just as starters, but you may join them together in combinations that please you and your loved ones and your time schedule.

COLD AVOCADO SOUP

A student of mine from Florida once brought me a giant avocado, straight from her tree. We let it ripen on the kitchen counter all week, and at week's end she whipped up a delightful no-cook soup. The secret to this recipe is using perfectly ripe avocados. The soup is delightful on a hot day and is beautiful in contrasting-color bowls. A dollop of fresh tomato salsa (page 28) is the perfect garnish.

2 ripe avocados, pitted and peeled

1 cup fresh or canned chicken stock or broth

1 cup heavy cream or sour cream

1 to 2 teaspoons chopped fresh cilantro

Juice of 1 lemon

Salt

Freshly ground black pepper

Chili pepper

Cut the avocados up roughly and place in a food processor or blender. Add the chicken stock and purée until smooth. Remove to a bowl and whisk in the cream or sour cream and cilantro. Season to taste with the lemon juice, salt, pepper, and chili pepper. Chill and serve.

Serves 4

RIPE AVOCADOS
One of the few vegetables that is virtually always served raw, avocados work well in many last-minute preparations. However, they should usually *not* be purchased at the last minute, as they are generally shipped to markets quite underripe when the delicate flesh is less susceptible to bruising. Place unripe avocados in a brown paper bag until the flesh yields to gentle pressure, checking daily; when ripe, refrigerate and use within 2 or 3 days.

STRAWBERRY SOUP

T his is truly a lazy chef's soup, just the ticket when the strawberries are ripe and sweet and it's too hot to bother about lunch. A few whirls of the blender or food processor and it's done, ready for delicate china or a Thermos for a picnic. As for all cold soups, starting with chilled ingredients reduces or eliminates the need to refrigerate before serving.

1 quart fresh strawberries, hulled

2 tablespoons honey

1 cup plain yogurt

1½ cups fresh orange juice

2 teaspoons finely grated orange peel (no white attached)

Purée the strawberries, in batches if necessary, in a blender or food processor. Transfer to a medium mixing bowl and stir in the honey, yogurt, orange juice, and peel. Refrigerate until well chilled. Serve cold.

Serves 4

ALL YOU NEED SOUP

PASTINA
This term refers to a broad category of small, shaped pastas that are often used in soup, ranging from tiny little stars and shells to short tubes and rice-shaped orzo. Their petite size allows them to cook more quickly than their larger counterparts, and they make wonderful side dishes for quick meals: boil, drain, and toss with some butter and grated Parmesan, or a bit of olive oil, fresh herbs, and chopped plum tomatoes.

My friend Margaret Ann Surber devised this restorative potion for a friend with a very bad cold. Although he couldn't taste a thing, it did the trick, and those of us who *were* healthy thought it was an incredibly delicious, satisfying soup, a meal in itself. It's important to use a small, quick-cooking pasta shape to avoid overcooking the vegetables and ruining the soup's fresh taste and bright colors.

2 tablespoons butter
1 medium onion, sliced
2 large carrots, peeled, quartered, and thinly sliced
1 large zucchini, quartered and thinly sliced
4 celery stalks, thinly sliced

6 cups canned or fresh chicken broth or stock, preferably fresh
3 to 4 cups cooked chicken
1 cup pastina (see sidebar)
Salt
Freshly ground black pepper
1 tablespoon chopped fresh thyme

Melt the butter in a large pot. Add the onion, carrots, zucchini, and celery and cook over low heat until soft, about 10 minutes. Add the stock and chicken to the pot, bring to a simmer, and add the pasta. Simmer until the pasta is cooked, 3 to 5 minutes. Season to taste with salt, pepper, and thyme.

Serves 6 to 8

CHILLED CITRUS-BLUEBERRY SOUP

You will love this refreshing, lowfat soup! Lemon balm is a mintlike herb that has a soft lemony flavor. It grows readily in my yard, where mint balks, but if mint is what you have, use it! You can eliminate the cooking step, and save even more time, if you use frozen sweetened blueberries, but in that case, omit the sugar. If your fresh blueberries are really sweet, purée them uncooked with some of the juice (omit the sugar) for a chunky, superquick variation.

½ pound blueberries, fresh or frozen, no sugar added
Grated peel (no white attached) and juice of 1 lemon
Grated peel (no white attached) and juice of 1 lime
Grated peel (no white attached) and juice of 1 orange
¼ cup sugar (optional)
½ teaspoon ground cinnamon

1 cup lowfat plain yogurt
¾ cup buttermilk
½ teaspoon almond extract

GARNISH
1 peach, peeled and chopped
1 tablespoon chopped fresh lemon balm or mint
¼ cup sour cream (optional)

Combine the blueberries, lemon peel and juice, lime peel and juice, orange peel and juice, sugar if using, and cinnamon in a medium saucepan. Bring to the boil. Then reduce the heat and simmer over medium-low heat, stirring occasionally, for about 10 minutes or until the blueberries are soft. Remove the solids to a food processor or blender with a slotted spoon, reserving the juice. Purée the solids, return to the saucepan with the juice, and cool (see sidebar). The soup may be made ahead to this point.

Mix the yogurt, buttermilk, and almond extract in a large bowl. Whisk in the cooled blueberry mixture, and chill until ready to serve. Garnish with peaches and lemon balm or mint and a dollop of sour cream if you are feeling decadent.

Serves 4

Note: The blueberry mixture can also be cooked for 3 to 4 minutes on High in the microwave, stirring once halfway through the cooking period.

CHILLED SOUPS
Cold soups are good choices for last-minute meals because they rarely require long cooking periods. They are also great make-ahead dishes, but if you don't have that luxury, be sure to start with ice-cold ingredients. To cool the finished soup down quickly, immerse the saucepan or bowl containing the soup in a large bowl or basin of water and ice for 10 minutes, stirring once or twice. Alternatively, transfer the soup to a resealable plastic bag, place flat on a baking sheet, and chill in the freezer.

BLACK BEAN GAZPACHO

CANNED BEANS

Purists will insist that canned beans don't measure up to their home-cooked dried equivalents, but there's no denying their convenience and versatility. I always keep cans of black beans, cannellinis, chickpeas, and Great Northerns on the shelf to stir into soups, chilis, salads, and healthy dips and spreads; just be sure to rinse off the sticky liquid they come packed in and drain well before using.

Black beans and tomatoes form the base of this chunky soup, which is served with an array of garnishes so that each diner can create his or her own masterpiece. If you refrigerate the cans of beans and tomato juice as well as the vegetables early in the day or even in the early evening, the soup will require little additional chilling.

2 15-ounce cans black beans

4 garlic cloves, peeled and very finely chopped

1/4 cup red wine vinegar

1/4 cup fresh lime juice (about 2 limes)

1 quart tomato juice, fresh or canned

2 cucumbers, peeled, seeded, and finely chopped

1 1/2 pounds very ripe tomatoes, peeled, seeded, and chopped or 1 28-ounce can Italian plum tomatoes, chopped

2 onions, finely chopped

Salt

Freshly ground black pepper

Sugar

G A R N I S H E S

1 cup sour cream

1 cup bread cubes, fried in 3 tablespoons olive oil until golden

1 tablespoon chopped fresh parsley

1 tablespoon chopped fresh cilantro (optional)

Drain and rinse the black beans and reserve in a large bowl. Add the garlic, red wine vinegar, lime juice, tomato juice, and one half of the cucumbers, tomatoes, and onions. Blend well and chill until ready to serve. Season to taste with salt, pepper, and a bit of sugar.

To serve, put the reserved chopped cucumber, tomato, and onion, as well as the additional garnishes, in small bowls and arrange around the soup.

Serves 8 to 10

Roasted Corn and Pepper Chowder

Here is a deeply flavored soup that doesn't cook for hours. Roasting the vegetables gives this colorful, Southwest-inspired soup a rich, smoky flavor, and although it adds another step (and a bit more time) the vegetables can roast as the chowder base simmers. You can also use vegetables grilled at another time and jarred red peppers to really speed things up. It's quite a substantial bowlful, but if all vegetables are not enough of a meal for you, add some grilled and chunked chicken, pork, or turkey.

2 onions, peeled and quartered

3 red bell peppers or ½ 12-ounce jar roasted red peppers

4 ears of corn, shucked

4 cups fresh or canned chicken stock or broth

1 potato, peeled and chopped

1½ teaspoons chopped fresh thyme

¼ teaspoon Tabasco sauce

¼ teaspoon red pepper flakes

Salt

Freshly ground black pepper

1 tablespoon chopped fresh cilantro

1 tablespoon fresh lime juice

Preheat the broiler.

Place the onions, bell peppers, and corn on a large baking sheet. Cook under the broiler until they are lightly charred, turning as needed, about 10 to 15 minutes. Cool the vegetables until they can be handled. Meanwhile, as the vegetables cook, heat the chicken stock, potato, thyme, Tabasco, and red pepper flakes in a large pot. Season to taste with salt and pepper. Bring to the boil. Simmer over medium heat for about 20 minutes or until the potato is tender.

Peel and seed the peppers, chop coarsely, and add to the soup. Chop the onions, cut the kernels from the corn cobs, and add to the soup. Heat through. Stir in the cilantro and lime juice and serve.

Serves 4

ROASTED VEGETABLES
Next time you barbecue, slice some extra vegetables, brush them lightly with oil, and throw them on the grill as the coals are dying down. You'll only need to turn them once, and you'll have a ready supply of delicious, smoky tidbits to stir into egg dishes, to top pizzas, or arrange on a platter and drizzle with olive oil, fresh thyme, and salt and pepper for an elegant, impromptu starter. Good choices for roasting are onions, fennel bulb, potatoes, red or yellow peppers, eggplants, and meaty mushrooms like Portobello, and zucchini.

FAST PANTRY PASTA E FAGIOLI

SOUP FROM LEFTOVERS
When you have only dribs and drabs left in the refrigerator, combine them with canned broth for a hearty minestrone-style soup. Many times, a little of this and that makes a soup you'll later wish you could duplicate! Just be sure to sniff everything you put in to be sure it isn't over the hill, and bring the soup to a good boil to rid it of bacteria, then reduce to a simmer and cook at least five minutes.

Every short-order cook needs a repertoire of soups that can be prepared start to finish in under 20 minutes. And if it is hearty enough to serve as a meal-in-a-bowl, better still. Drained beans provide protein and fiber in this classic Italian preparation. If you don't have all the ingredients called for, simply leave them out or substitute what you do have in the pantry or crisper. You can cook the pasta separately and add it to the soup base just to heat through, a good idea if you are planning to have leftovers, as pasta can be easily overcooked.

1 tablespoon olive oil

2 onions, chopped

2 garlic cloves, peeled and chopped

2 carrots, peeled and shredded

1 roasted red bell pepper, chopped

8 cups fresh or canned chicken stock or broth, boiling

1 16-ounce can tomato wedges, undrained

1 cup dried pasta shells

1 15-ounce can chickpeas, drained and rinsed

1 16-ounce can kidney beans, drained and rinsed

1 teaspoon black pepper

1 tablespoon poultry seasoning

¼ teaspoon cayenne pepper (optional)

Salt

In a 3½-quart Dutch oven, heat the olive oil over medium heat. Add the onions, garlic, carrots, and red bell pepper and cook until soft, about 5 minutes. Add the boiling stock, tomato wedges, pasta, chickpeas, kidney beans, pepper, poultry seasoning, and cayenne pepper if using. Season to taste with salt. Cook over medium heat until the pasta is cooked, but still firm, 5 to 9 minutes.

Serves 6 to 8

VEGETARIAN GUMBO

This soup can be a hearty starter or stand on its own as an all-in-one meal. I've added leftover cooked chicken, sausage, and shrimp to stretch it, but drained canned crab would work equally well, although any of these additions belie the recipe's name. The rich, zesty gumbo broth cries out for an accompaniment of crusty bread. This soup freezes and reheats well.

3 tablespoons vegetable oil

1 large onion, chopped

3 garlic cloves, peeled and finely chopped

1 pound okra, cut into ½-inch-thick slices

½ green bell pepper, cut into ¼-inch pieces

1 14-ounce can whole tomatoes, broken up with a spoon

¼ cup chopped fresh parsley

1 bay leaf

3 tablespoons finely chopped fresh basil

1 19-ounce can chickpeas, drained

1 cup vegetable stock or water

1 teaspoon salt

1 tablespoon fresh lemon juice

Dash of Tabasco sauce (optional)

4 cups cooked rice

In a large pot, heat the oil over medium heat. Add the onion and cook until soft and translucent, about 3 to 5 minutes. Add the garlic, okra, and bell pepper, and cook 5 to 8 minutes. Add the tomatoes, parsley, bay leaf, and basil. Reduce the heat to simmer and cook until the okra is soft, 10 to 15 minutes. Add the chickpeas, vegetable stock, salt, and lemon juice, and heat thoroughly; discard the bay leaf. Add hot sauce to taste if desired. Serve over the rice.

Serves 4 to 6

PRECHOPPED GARLIC

This convenience product does save time, and there are now many good types of chopped garlic available. It is essential to keep it refrigerated, as harmful bacteria can develop at room temperature. Different brands use different preservatives, so buy a small quantity to taste. One teaspoon of prechopped garlic equals one garlic clove, chopped.

SPINACH SOUP

I recently discovered a bunch of slightly wilted spinach in my refrigerator. Instead of fussing with culling the less than perfect leaves, I decided to make a wonderful nutritious soup! It is really beautiful puréed but may certainly also be served without that extra step.

1 tablespoon olive oil
2 leeks, white and pale green parts only,
  cut into ¼-inch slices
1 potato, peeled and cut into ½-inch
  pieces
1 bay leaf

3 to 4 cups fresh or canned chicken stock
  or broth or water
¼ pound fresh spinach, trimmed
Salt
Freshly ground black pepper
¼ cup heavy cream or plain yogurt

In a large Dutch oven, heat the olive oil over medium-high heat. Add the leeks and cook without browning until translucent, 3 to 4 minutes. Add the potato, bay leaf, and 3 cups of the chicken stock, and bring to the boil. Reduce the heat, cover, and simmer until the vegetables are tender, 10 to 15 minutes. Add more stock if necessary. Add the spinach and simmer, uncovered, just until the spinach is cooked and bright green, 3 to 5 minutes. Season to taste with salt and pepper. Remove the bay leaf. If desired, transfer the solids to a food processor or blender, purée in batches (if necessary) until smooth. Return to the pot, add the heavy cream if using, and return to the boil. If using yogurt, stir into the hot soup just before serving. Adjust salt and pepper to taste and serve piping hot.

Serves 4 to 6

WHITE BEAN OR LENTIL AND SAUSAGE SOUP

I enjoy this soup by itself, with a salad and bread, or as a base to which I add sliced cooked carrots, greens, green peas, and/or chopped tomatoes, depending on what I have available, in the last 5 minutes. It's thick and lusty, almost like a stew, and extremely satisfying.

ABOUT LENTILS
Lentils are the legume of choice for time-conscious cooks, as they require no pre-soaking and cook in under a half hour. Cook them in boiling water (don't salt) to cover by at least an inch until tender, checking frequently; don't overcook or they will turn to mush. Try green, red, and brown French lentils for visual variety in your dishes. Canned lentils are an acceptable substitute if you can't spare even that much time.

½ pound sweet Italian sausage, cut in
1-inch pieces
1 onion, chopped
2 garlic cloves, peeled and chopped
2 cups fresh or canned chicken stock or broth

2 15-ounce cans white beans or lentils
1 tablespoon chopped fresh rosemary
¼ cup sherry
Salt
Freshly ground black pepper

In a heavy 2-quart casserole, cook the sausage on low to medium heat until much of the fat has been rendered, 4 or 5 minutes. Turn up the heat and cook until light brown. Add the onion and garlic and cook until soft, 4 to 6 minutes, draining off some of the fat as necessary. Add the stock and beans with their liquid. Bring to the boil, reduce the heat, add the rosemary, and simmer 5 to 10 minutes. Add the sherry, cook for a moment, and add salt and pepper to taste.

Serves 4

BASIC VINAIGRETTE

This recipe is a springboard for many different salad dressings. Just changing the vinegar or type of mustard or oil gives the vinaigrette a markedly different character. Substitute a hot mustard to toss with wilted greens or other Asian salads, or use part walnut oil to dress a pear and blue cheese salad. The ratio of oil to vinegar, however, should always remain three to one.

¼ cup red wine vinegar
1 teaspoon Dijon mustard
1 garlic clove, peeled and very finely
  chopped

¾ cup vegetable oil
Salt
Freshly ground black pepper
Pinch of sugar (optional)

In a medium-size bowl, whisk together the vinegar, mustard, and garlic until well combined. Slowly drizzle the oil into the mixture in a steady stream, whisking constantly until emulsified. Season to taste with salt and pepper and add a small pinch of sugar to tone down the acidity if necessary.

Makes 1 cup

TARRAGON MAYONNAISE

Store-bought mayonnaise can be dressed up easily with a splash of tarragon and a bit of tarragon vinegar. Try this in potato, egg, or grain salads.

1 egg yolk
½ tablespoon tarragon vinegar or lemon
  juice
¾ cup olive oil

1 tablespoon chopped fresh tarragon
  leaves
Salt
White pepper

In a food processor, combine the egg yolk and vinegar. With the motor running, add the oil in a thin steady stream. Stir in the tarragon. Season to taste with salt and pepper.

Makes 1 cup

APPLE WALDORF CHICKEN SALAD

In my home the evening meal is quite often a salad. This creamy, chunky blend is a welcome variation on the chicken salad of my youth, with a bit more punch from the mustard. Any cooked chicken will do, so if you have leftovers, they will work fine. Add raisins if you like.

2 cups fresh or canned chicken stock or
*   broth*
1 bay leaf
1 garlic clove, peeled and finely chopped
4 chicken breasts, cut into 1- to 1½-
*   inch pieces*
1 cup mayonnaise

1 tablespoon Dijon mustard
½ cup walnut halves
2 Granny Smith apples, cored and cut
*   into ½-inch pieces*
Salt
White pepper

In a medium-size pan, heat the chicken stock, bay leaf, and garlic to a simmer. Add the chicken breast pieces and return to a simmer. Poach until done, about 5 to 8 minutes. Remove the chicken and place on a baking sheet or plate to cool. Save the stock for another use.

While the chicken is cooling, combine the mayonnaise, mustard, walnuts, and apples in a large bowl. When the chicken has cooled sufficiently, add it to the dressing. Season to taste with salt and pepper. Serve immediately or chill.

Serves 6 to 8

COLD SALMON AND ALMOND SALAD

Here is a light and wonderful use for leftover or canned salmon for a summer lunch or supper or for a Sunday night supper any time. Accompany it with fresh asparagus and parslied orzo. If possible, use one of the sweet onions, such as Vidalia or Walla Walla, otherwise use a red onion or green onions.

1 cucumber, peeled and seeded, chopped into ¼-inch cubes

1 small sweet onion such as Vidalia, Texas Sweet, or Walla Walla, finely chopped

2 tablespoons finely chopped fresh parsley

½ cup toasted sliced almonds

3 tablespoons Tarragon Mayonnaise (page 43)

Chopped peel (no white attached) of 1 lemon

Juice of 1 lemon

2 cups cooked salmon, flaked (or 2 8-ounce cans, drained and bones removed)

Salt

Freshly ground black pepper

In a medium bowl, combine the cucumber, onion, parsley, sliced almond, mayonnaise, lemon peel, and lemon juice. Gently fold in the salmon. Season to taste with salt and pepper and chill until ready to serve.

Serves 4

LACY GREEN SALAD

When all is said and done, a simple green salad is often the only perfect accompaniment to a meal. Any combination of greens can be used to vary the color, flavors, and textures as you desire.

SALAD INTO ENTRÉE
If you are transforming a green salad into a more substantial luncheon or supper dish with the addition of sliced grilled meat, chicken, or fish, some canned tuna or salmon, or sliced hard-cooked eggs and beefsteak tomatoes, toss the more substantial ingredients with the dressing in a mixing bowl, then spoon over the greens.

¼ head curly endive or frisée
¼ head escarole
½ head leaf lettuce, red or green
¼ cup red wine vinegar
½ teaspoon Dijon mustard

1 garlic clove, peeled and finely chopped
⅓ cup oil
Salt
Freshly ground black pepper

Wash and dry the endive, escarole, and leaf lettuce and tear into large pieces. Whisk together the vinegar, mustard, and garlic with the oil. Season to taste with salt and pepper. When ready to serve, pour over lettuce.

Serves 4 to 6

WATERCRESS AND BACON SALAD

Few things are more appealing or easier than a salad of watercress topped with a simple vinaigrette—especially if the watercress is washed and the bacon fried ahead of time. The bitter flavor of the watercress, the tang of the vinaigrette, and the crispy crunch of the red onion and bacon all work together to make a nice foil for lamb or poultry.

VINAIGRETTE
3 tablespoons white wine vinegar or
*   champagne vinegar*
⅓ cup olive oil
2 teaspoons Dijon mustard
Salt
Freshly ground black pepper

2 bunches watercress, washed and
*   stemmed*
4 slices bacon, fried, drained on paper
*   towels, and finely crumbled*
½ red onion, finely chopped

In a small mixing bowl, whisk together the vinegar, oil, and Dijon mustard. Add salt and pepper to taste.

Arrange the watercress on plates. Sprinkle with the bacon and red onion. Top each serving with a little of the vinaigrette.

Serves 4

Variation: Top the watercress with ½ pound scallops that have been lightly poached and sprinkle with a vinaigrette of ⅓ cup lime juice and ½ cup olive oil.

WARM BROCCOLI-MUSHROOM SALAD

A warm salad is just a little different and can serve as a salad or a vegetable. The bacon provides a smoky flavor and the pungent raspberry vinegar is so sweet that no oil is necessary. Use just a touch, as the heat intensifies the vinegar's flavor. This recipe is a great way to use broccoli leftovers and takes only minutes if you use presliced mushrooms.

1 head broccoli or 1 12-ounce package frozen broccoli, cut into bite-size florets
3 slices bacon, cut into bits

1 medium onion, finely chopped
2 tablespoons raspberry or balsamic vinegar
½ pound mushrooms, sliced

Cook the broccoli according to microwave directions or steam the florets over boiling water until just crisp-tender. Rinse with cold water and set aside to cool. In a large skillet over medium heat, cook the bacon until most of the fat is rendered. Add the onion and cook until soft and the bacon is crisp, 2 to 3 minutes. Add the raspberry vinegar, bring to the boil, and reduce by half. Remove from the heat. Add the mushrooms and broccoli and toss to coat. Serve immediately while slightly warm.

Serves 4 to 6

Shredded Carrot Slaw with Poppy Seed Vinaigrette

Sweet carrots, pineapple, and raisins contrast nicely with a savory vinaigrette in this offbeat slaw. Adapt this formula to suit your own tastes: currants instead of raisins, pecans instead of walnuts, green onions instead of shallots, or sesame seeds instead of poppy seeds are all perfectly delicious substitutions. Its flavor will be even better if you have time to let it chill for an hour or two.

CHILLING SALADS
To speed up the chilling time, spread shredded salads like cole slaw on a metal baking sheet or jelly roll pan and refrigerate. This also works for washed and dried lettuce leaves; cover with a damp kitchen towel or paper towels.

6 carrots, shredded

1 20-ounce can pineapple chunks, drained

1/2 cup golden raisins

1/2 cup chopped toasted walnuts

3 tablespoons chopped fresh parsley

2 teaspoons Dijon mustard

1 tablespoon sugar

2 tablespoons finely chopped shallots

1/3 cup apple cider vinegar

3 tablespoons peanut oil

2 tablespoons poppy seeds

1/2 teaspoon ground cinnamon

Salt

Freshly ground black pepper

8 lettuce leaves

In a large bowl, toss together the carrots, pineapple chunks, raisins, walnuts, and parsley. In a measuring cup, whisk together the Dijon mustard, sugar, shallots, vinegar, peanut oil, poppy seeds, and cinnamon. Season to taste with salt and pepper. Pour over the carrot mixture, toss, and chill if possible. Serve on lettuce leaves.

Serves 6 to 8

CAULIFLOWER WITH HERBED VINAIGRETTE

STORING CAULIFLOWER

Prevent cauliflower from "going brown" by storing it in your refrigerator stem-side up, in an open plastic bag. Poke a few holes in the bag so air can circulate. Or, turn stem-side up in a shallow container of water.

Cauliflower has a reputation for being a bit bland, but studded with red peppers, herbs, and onions it makes a pretty salad with a lot of interest and flavor. It is a lovely buffet item. Use jarred peppers and prechopped garlic to speed the dish along. The cauliflower can be cooked up to 2 days in advance, in which case this is a snap to put together.

1 medium head cauliflower (about 2½ pounds)
Salt
1 red bell pepper, roasted, peeled, seeded, and cut into strips
1 red onion, thinly sliced
3 green onions, sliced
2 teaspoons Dijon mustard
2 garlic cloves, peeled and chopped

¼ cup white wine vinegar
½ cup olive oil
Freshly ground black pepper
Sugar
2 tablespoons finely chopped fresh parsley
1 tablespoon finely chopped fresh dill
½ teaspoon celery seeds

Break the cauliflower into florets and rinse. In a 3-quart stockpot, bring a large quantity of salted water to the boil. Add the cauliflower and cook until crisp-tender, 4 to 5 minutes. Drain and rinse under cold water. In a large bowl, toss together the cauliflower, red pepper, red onion, and green onions. In a small bowl, mix together the Dijon mustard, garlic, and wine vinegar. Slowly add the olive oil, whisking to make an emulsion. Season to taste with salt, pepper, and sugar. Mix together the parsley, dill, and celery seeds. Stir into the vinaigrette and pour over the vegetables. Serve chilled or at room temperature.

Serves 6 to 8

CHILLED PINE NUT AND CELERY COUSCOUS SALAD

Quick-cooking couscous is the busy cook's savior. Dressed up with pine nuts, dried fruit, and an exotic vinaigrette, it's almost a meal in itself, and its mideastern flavors make it a delicious accompaniment to salmon, chicken, or lamb.

2¼ cups fresh or canned chicken stock or
   broth, heated to the boil

1¾ cups couscous

1 tablespoon olive oil

½ cup pine nuts

2 celery stalks, chopped

6 green onions, chopped, green part only

1 cup currants or raisins

DRESSING

½ cup fresh lemon juice

2 tablespoons olive oil

1 teaspoon ground cinnamon

1 teaspoon freshly ground black pepper

1 teaspoon turmeric

Salt

In a heatproof bowl, pour the boiling chicken stock over the couscous and set aside until the broth has all been absorbed.

Heat the oil in a large skillet. Add the pine nuts and sauté until golden, about 3 to 5 minutes. Add the celery, green onions, and currants and cook for 1 minute longer. Stir into the couscous.

In a small bowl combine the lemon juice, olive oil, cinnamon, black pepper, turmeric, and salt to taste. Blend well and toss with the couscous. Serve chilled or at room temperature.

Serves 6 to 8

COUSCOUS TERMINOLOGY
Couscous is now being sold in a confusing way. Both the modern processed "quick-cooking" couscous, which requires only hot liquid poured over it and a brief soaking to swell up and be "cooked," and the traditional couscous, which takes longer to cook, are sold as couscous. The only way to know for sure which you are buying is to check the cooking directions on the package. The traditional couscous is not available in most grocery stores.

Pear and Blue Cheese Salad

I always find salads that combine cheese and fruit rather elegant, a pleasant starter for a special meal. If the lettuce is washed and dried ahead and the pecans already toasted and chopped, all that needs to be done is to slice the pears and plate the salads, quick and easy enough for weeknight entertaining.

To make this great salad even better, use an imported blue cheese such as Stilton or Saga. If you like, the salads can be topped with crispy bacon bits, about 6 strips, fried, drained, and crumbled.

6 leaves red leaf lettuce

6 pears, halved, cored, and cut into thin wedges

2 to 3 tablespoons balsamic vinegar

$\frac{1}{2}$ cup blue cheese, crumbled

$\frac{1}{2}$ cup pecans, toasted and coarsely chopped

3 green onions, sliced

Freshly ground black pepper

$\frac{1}{4}$ cup grated or shaved imported Parmesan cheese (optional)

Place a lettuce leaf on each of 6 plates. Divide the pear wedges among the plates. Drizzle the balsamic vinegar over the pears, then sprinkle each salad with the blue cheese, pecans, green onions, pepper, and the Parmesan if using. Serve at once.

Serves 6

Green Salad with Apples and Parmesan Vinaigrette

This is a very colorful, crunchy salad. The slight bitterness of the greens contrasts nicely with the sweetness of the apples, pears, and raisins, and the tang of the vinaigrette ties the whole combination together for a truly unique, refreshing side dish. You might want to make it a whole meal with the addition of julienned, thinly sliced ham.

1 apple, red or green

1 ripe pear

2 tablespoons fresh lemon juice

1 head red leaf lettuce, torn into 2-inch
  pieces

1 head radicchio, torn into 2-inch
  pieces

1/2 red onion, sliced thin

1/2 cup golden raisins

2 tablespoons chopped fresh parsley

1/3 cup toasted walnuts

PARMESAN VINAIGRETTE

1/4 cup red wine vinegar

1 to 2 garlic cloves, peeled and chopped

1/2 tablespoon Dijon mustard

1/4 cup grated imported Parmesan cheese

1/2 cup olive oil

Salt

Freshly ground black pepper

Sugar

2 ounces shaved imported Parmesan cheese

Core the apple and pear and cut into 1-inch pieces. Place in a large bowl, sprinkle with the lemon juice, and toss to coat (this prevents them from turning brown). Add the red leaf lettuce, radicchio, red onion, raisins, parsley, and toasted walnuts, and toss well.

For the vinaigrette, in a food processor or blender, purée the red wine vinegar, garlic, Dijon, and grated Parmesan until smooth. With the machine running, add the olive oil in a slow stream to make an emulsion. Season to taste with salt, pepper, and sugar. Pour over the salad and toss again. Top with the shaved Parmesan and serve.

Serves 6 to 8

ORIENTAL SALAD WITH SESAME SOY VINAIGRETTE

SPEEDING SLAWS

A food processor with a julienning blade or a mandoline (a slicing device with adjustable blades) makes quick work of shredding carrots and other hard vegetables for cole slaws and salads, tedious work to do by hand. For cabbage, spinach, or lettuce, cut out any tough core or remove the stems, stack the leaves in a pile, and cut quickly across the stack to make fine strips.

The Oriental section of grocery stores brings incredible diversity to my table. I'm amazed at the range of rice vinegars alone, and what a welcome addition they are. Oriental sesame oil is a shiny, dark oil, quite different from its pale counterpart; a little goes a long way. Napa cabbage is a crinkly, elongated cabbage related to Chinese cabbage. You may want to use perfumy enoki mushrooms for an even more Oriental mood.

I substitute other vegetables in this—seeing what's left over (after I've sliced everything in advance) at the end of the week. This salad will happily accommodate cooked shrimp or slices of grilled salmon, chicken, or beef.

SALAD

1 cup fresh spinach, cut in julienne strips

½ cup cabbage, preferably Napa, cut in julienne strips (discard tough center rib or stem)

3 green onions, cut in 2-inch lengths

1 to 2 carrots, peeled, cut in 2-inch julienne strips

¼ cup sliced button mushrooms

1 4-ounce can sliced water chestnuts, drained

SESAME SOY VINAIGRETTE

¼ cup vegetable oil

¼ cup rice vinegar or rice wine vinegar

1½ tablespoons dark sesame oil

2 tablespoons soy sauce

Salt

Freshly ground black pepper

½ teaspoon sugar

GARNISH

2 tablespoons sesame seeds

In a large bowl, toss together the spinach, Napa cabbage, green onions, carrots, mushrooms, and water chestnuts.

In a small bowl, whisk together the oil, rice vinegar, sesame oil, and soy sauce. Season to taste with salt and pepper. Add the sugar and mix well. Toss the salad with the dressing and top with sesame seeds.

Serves 4

Vegetables in Lemon Vinaigrette

This colorful and simply prepared dish will jazz up everyday suppers. It is nothing if not adaptable; you can use the fresh herbs of your own choosing and vary the vegetables to reflect your main course as well as the season or what's in your vegetable bin. My grocery store has matchstick carrots and broccoli stems for sale, which work well in this recipe too. Serve this at room temperature or chill, if you prefer and have the time.

3 carrots, cut into 3-inch matchsticks

2 cups cauliflower, cut into florets

1 pound Brussels sprouts, tough outer leaves removed and a small X cut into each bottom

LEMON VINAIGRETTE

1 tablespoon olive oil

½ cup fresh lemon juice

1 teaspoon Dijon mustard

2 garlic cloves, peeled and chopped

¼ cup chopped fresh parsley, basil, oregano, and/or thyme

Salt

Freshly ground black pepper

1 red bell pepper, thinly sliced

Steam the carrots, cauliflower, and Brussels sprouts over boiling water until crisp-tender, about 8 minutes. Drain and refresh under cold water.

In a small bowl, combine the olive oil, lemon juice, mustard, garlic, and fresh herbs, and season to taste with salt and pepper. Whisk until well combined and set aside.

Place the vegetables in a large bowl, add the red pepper and the vinaigrette, toss to coat, and serve.

Serves 6 to 8

STEAMING VERSUS BLANCHING

For salads and other dishes where partially cooked or crisp-tender vegetables are desired, blanching in a generous amount of boiling water is generally the preferred cooking method. When time is tight, however, steaming is the better choice, as it takes far less time to bring an inch of water to the boil in a steamer than it does a full pot of water. I confess I use an electric steamer, and I find it saves me a great deal of time. Also, consider microwaving vegetables in a tightly covered container for 3 or 4 minutes. They can be refreshed under cold water to stop them from cooking further.

Clams in a Cataplana Casa Velha ■ Basic Broiled or Grilled Fish with Lemon or Lime ■ Baked Fish with Garlic and Vinegar ■ Fillets of Fish Steamed with Limes and Cilantro on Cucumber Noodles ■ Halibut with Gingered Vegetables ■ Skewered Oysters ■ Salt-Crusted Pompano ■ Salmon with Mustard ■ Oriental Baked Salmon ■ Eighteen-Minute Herbed Scallops ■ Beautiful Shrimp or Scallop Stir-Fry ■ Sesame-Ginger Fried Shrimp ■ Broiled Scallops with Parmesan ■ Patti's Trout with Pistachio Crust

FISH AND FOWL

3

■ Uncle John's Ginger Tuna Steak ■ Chicken Breasts with Apples and Cheese ■ Basic Grilled or Broiled Chicken Breasts ■ Blackberry Chicken ■ Salsa Chicken ■ Roaster Breast with Cranberry Relish ■ Tarragon Chicken ■ Turmeric Sesame Chicken ■ Simple Casserole Chicken ■ Chicken, Tomato, and Vegetable Fricassee ■ Broiled Lemon Rosemary Chicken ■ Chicken with Rutabaga and Potatoes ■ Chicken with Dried Cherries ■ Chicken Provence ■ Thai Thighs ■ Cornish Hens ■ Lee Anne's Savory Quail

FISH, SHELLFISH, BONELESS chicken cutlets—what would the time-challenged cook do without these fast-cooking, endlessly variable staples? They can be dressed up or down, defrosted in a flash if you've thought to stockpile them in the freezer, and have the added advantage of being lower in fat than many other protein sources. And don't forget that leftovers can be recycled into an alluring array of salads, pastas, and other spur-of-the-moment creations.

When I was growing up the only fish we ate was what we'd caught ourselves, or mealy frozen fish sticks. Fortunately, that's no longer the case, with even the smaller local fish markets offering a veritable feast of fresh or flash frozen and defrosted seafood. Fish and shellfish also tend to be among the priciest dinner options, although buying what's in season helps. However, they are worth their weight in gold when you are really pushed, particularly for entertaining. In fact, I frequently find that fish cooks too fast for me to get everything else done at the same time. This is when a timetable is especially helpful, ensuring that the dish that requires the longest cooking time will be started first. Thicker fish steaks or preparations that add thickness in the form of breading, a crust, or cooking bed, give me more control (don't forget the Canadian rule for cooking fish of 10 minutes per inch of thickness), and in the long run, make it easier to avoid a disaster if everything else isn't ready.

Poultry is, of course, the other busy day standby. Today, savvy poultry producers are packaging chicken specifically with the needs of busy cooks in mind; you will find everything from small whole chicken and Cornish hens to boned thigh meat, roaster parts, and even cubed, boneless breast meat. Since modern chicken often does not have a particularly assertive flavor, it accommodates itself to various flavor enhancing ingredients; with a chicken and a few choice pantry ingredients or fresh vegetables to throw into the casserole it is a surety that one's family will never go hungry. Bear in mind, too, that recipes for chicken are easily interchangeable with other poultry—turkey having a somewhat stronger flavor and quails and Cornish hens a more uptown presentation.

Whichever parts you prefer, chicken in the freezer, or fish from the market, as well as inexpensive canned fish such as crab, shrimp, clams and even good old tuna, will form the base of interesting and sophisticated dishes and generally provide panic insurance.

Clams in a Cataplana Casa Velha

I had this for the first time in a charming little port town in Portugal when my old high school chum Lucia and I went there in the early 90s. We were served from the cataplana—a flat-bottomed copper bowl hinged with a copper lid—and ate watching the boats come in. However, if a regular casserole dish is used, it will be every bit as delicious. The sauce cooks quickly but may also be made ahead (add the clams at the last minute), so it's ideal for a fast meal. And it's so exciting visually! The sauce begs to be mopped up with a French-type bread. This dish would also be very nice over linguini.

2 dozen littleneck or other small clams

2 tablespoons olive oil

1 tablespoon butter

1½ medium onions, thinly sliced

1 large green bell pepper, cored, seeded, and cut into thin strips

2 garlic cloves, peeled and chopped

1 small bay leaf

½ pound fresh or canned tomatoes with liquid

1 4-ounce can tomato sauce

1½ ounces smoked ham, cut in small cubes

¼ cup dry white wine or chicken broth (optional)

GARNISH

¼ cup coarsely chopped fresh Italian parsley (optional)

CLEANING CLAMS
Don't let the tough shells of clams intimidate you! They're quite simple to clean, and the opened clams in their shells always make a lovely presentation. I find the following steps to be the best method:

Place the clams in a large bowl, cover with cold water, and scrub well with a vegetable brush to remove the dirt. Toss the clams around with your hands and shake off the excess grit. Lift the clams out of the water, discard the water, and rinse the bowl. Repeat this procedure until there is no more sediment in the bottom of the bowl, once or twice more.

Scrub the clams well in cool water. Heat the olive oil and butter in a large skillet over moderate heat, add the onions and green pepper, and sauté until softened and golden, about 10 minutes. Add the garlic and sauté for another 2 to 3 minutes. Add the bay leaf, tomatoes and their liquid, and tomato sauce. Break up the tomatoes and bring the mixture to a simmer. Add the smoked ham, cover, and simmer for 10 to 15 minutes. *The sauce can be made ahead to this point and refrigerated up to 2 days.*

When ready to cook the clams, spoon the sauce into a cataplana or a deep

Dutch oven and bring to a simmer. Add the clams, cover tightly, and cook over medium heat, shaking occasionally, until the clams open, about 10 to 15 minutes. Add the optional wine or chicken broth if you would like a thinner sauce and heat through. Ladle into shallow bowls and sprinkle with parsley.

Serves 2 as a main course; 4 as a starter

BASIC BROILED OR GRILLED FISH WITH LEMON OR LIME

Broiling or grilling is probably the quickest way to cook fish. Thin fillets, such as flounder and sole, will be ready in 2 to 4 minutes, while thicker pieces, such as grouper, tuna, salmon, or monkfish steaks or fillets, require 10 minutes to the inch of thickness. For either grilling or broiling it is best to leave the skin on the fish to make turning the fillet easier, but do cut 1- to 2¼-inch slits in the skin to prevent buckling and aid in cooking. If the fillet is skinless and you are concerned it will break, you need not turn it at all, but do protect the fillet with a thin coating of oil or butter.

4 fish fillets (1¼ to 1½ pounds)
2 tablespoons butter, melted, or oil
Salt
Freshly ground black pepper
¼ cup fresh lemon or lime juice

1 tablespoon fresh chopped herbs, such as rosemary, thyme, oregano, basil, or chives (optional)
½ teaspoon paprika (optional)

Dip the fillets in the butter or oil. Place on a foil-lined baking sheet. Measure the fillets' thickness and broil until done, 10 minutes to the inch of thickness, turning halfway through the cooking time, if possible. When done transfer to a warm platter using a spatula or pancake turner and season with salt and pepper. Drizzle the lemon or lime juice over the fillets and sprinkle with the herbs and paprika if using.

Serves 4

BAKED FISH WITH GARLIC AND VINEGAR

Late one afternoon I read *Flavors of Greece* by Rosemary Barron and got a craving for the Baked Fish with Garlic and Vinegar. Alas, I was unable to buy a whole fish, but I found that substituting fillets did not diminish the extraordinarily exciting presentation with whole sprigs of fresh rosemary, whole garlic cloves, and cracked pepper. You'll smell the Mediterranean when this dish comes out of the oven. Be sure to serve bread to mop up this fantastic sauce.

6 fillets of rainbow trout, red snapper, tilapia, or other mild fish, preferably skinned

Salt

¾ tablespoon cracked pepper

¼ cup olive oil

1½ tablespoons butter

24 garlic cloves, peeled

1 medium onion, sliced

6 sprigs fresh rosemary

2 bay leaves

3 tablespoons red wine vinegar

Preheat the oven to 400°F. Lightly grease a 9 × 13-inch baking dish or a large baking sheet.

Dry the fish with paper towels and rub both sides of the fillets with salt to taste and all the pepper. Set aside.

Heat 2 tablespoons of the oil and the butter in a large frying pan. Add the garlic and onion and sauté until brown, about 10 minutes. Measure the fillets. If they're not 1 inch thick, fold them in half or thirds, making them as close to 1 inch thick as possible, and place them in the baking dish. Top with rosemary and bay leaves. Cover with the sautéed garlic and onion. Whisk together the remaining 2 tablespoons olive oil and the red wine vinegar. Pour half of this mixture over the fish, bake 5 minutes, then pour the remaining mixture over the fish and bake until fish flakes easily, 5 to 7 minutes longer. Total baking time should be 10 minutes per inch of thickness. Remove the bay leaves and serve hot.

Serves 6

FILLETS OF FISH STEAMED WITH LIMES AND CILANTRO ON CUCUMBER NOODLES

I often have a cucumber or two in my vegetable bin, bought for a salad but then forgotten. This technique is a whimsical way to use them, even if they're not quite up to salad quality anymore. The pared cucumber looks like pasta, hence the name of this innovative dish. Trout, tilapia, grouper, and red snapper are among the fish ideally suited to this dish. The cilantro adds a wonderful touch. You can also substitute lemons for limes if you prefer. Obviously sesame oil and soy sauce are not interchangeable, but either works.

4 trout, tilapia, grouper, or red snapper
   fillets
Juice of 2 limes
1 teaspoon Oriental sesame oil or soy
   sauce
2 tablespoons chopped fresh cilantro or
   chopped fresh ginger

Salt
Freshly ground black pepper
2 cucumbers, peeled, halved lengthwise,
   and seeded

GARNISH
1 lime, cut into wedges

Arrange the fillets in a heatproof dish. Cover the fillets with the lime juice, sesame oil, and cilantro, and season to taste with salt and pepper. Place over a pot of simmering water, cover, and steam until the fish is opaque throughout, about 10 minutes.

While the fish steams, use a vegetable peeler to pare long strips from each cucumber half. Sprinkle them with salt, place in a strainer, and set aside for 10 minutes to drain. (This step can be omitted in a pinch.) Rinse them, squeeze out the moisture, and mound on 4 plates.

Place a fillet on each cucumber "noodle" bed and garnish with lime wedges.

Serves 4

HALIBUT WITH GINGERED VEGETABLES

A recent trip to Alaska made me a halibut lover. It's a lovely moist fish that has an affinity for Asian ingredients. Each oval steak is bisected by a single cross–shaped bone that is easily cut out, leaving 4 equal, boneless portions. Don't hesitate to buy frozen halibut; much of what we buy as "fresh" was in fact previously frozen, and it's handy to keep as a freezer staple.

1 tablespoon vegetable oil

2 1-inch-thick halibut steaks, about 8 ounces each

1 tablespoon finely chopped fresh ginger

1 tablespoon soy sauce

1 to 2 tablespoons sherry (optional)

½ cup finely julienned red bell pepper

1 carrot, peeled and cut into ribbons

2 tablespoons daikon, peeled and cut into ribbons

½ cup snow peas

¼ cup bean sprouts

Cellophane noodles

Heat the vegetable oil in a large skillet over high heat. Cut each fish steak away from the bone and into 4 pieces; pat dry. Add the fish to the skillet and cook 5 to 8 minutes. After 5 minutes turn the fish and add the ginger, soy sauce, sherry if using, red bell pepper, carrot ribbons, and daikon ribbons. Simmer 5 minutes to cook the vegetables slightly. (The fish should cook a total of 10 minutes per inch of thickness; if it is done before the vegetables, transfer to a warmed plate while the vegetables finish cooking.) Add the snow peas and bean sprouts and cook 2 minutes longer. Toss well to coat the vegetables with the sauce. Serve with cellophane noodles.

Serves 4

NOTE: *Daikon is a large, white, mild-flavored root vegetable that is widely available at Oriental grocery stores, organic food stores, and many farmers' markets.*

SKEWERED OYSTERS

The delicate texture of oysters benefits from just the briefest cooking, and since a simple presentation is often the best way to enhance their smoky sweetness, they are super last-minute fare. These go well on a bed of rice, pasta, or couscous, but could also be served as an appetizer. If using wooden skewers, be sure to soak them in water before threading to keep them from burning.

½ cup (1 stick) butter, melted

3 garlic cloves, peeled and finely chopped

24 oysters, shucked

Salt

Freshly ground black pepper

1½ tablespoons chopped fresh parsley

1½ tablespoons chopped fresh thyme

Tabasco sauce

Horseradish

Preheat the grill or broiler.

Mix together the butter and garlic and toss the oysters in the mixture. Thread the oysters on small skewers and place them on a hot grill or on a baking sheet 6 inches from a hot broiler. Cook until the oysters turn white and are starting to curl at the edges, about 5 to 8 minutes.

Season to taste with salt and pepper. Sprinkle with the chopped herbs. Serve with Tabasco sauce and horseradish as desired. You can leave the oysters on the skewers for an informal presentation or remove them to plates.

Serves 4

NOTE: *If you prefer to serve the oysters on toothpicks, omit the skewers, spread the oysters on a baking sheet, and broil as above.*

SALT-CRUSTED POMPANO

Don't let the brevity of the ingredient list fool you: This is an exceptionally flavorful way to prepare fish, and it makes a really exciting and unusual presentation when you crack the crust at the table. (If you are not that confident, do it in the kitchen just before serving.) The substantial crust steams the fish in its own juices for a very moist result.

Kosher (coarse) salt
1 2- to 3-pound pompano, cleaned, fins
   trimmed

Freshly ground black pepper

Preheat the oven to 350°F. Cover a baking sheet with a ¼-inch layer of kosher salt.

Pat the fish dry. Season on each side with pepper to taste. Place the fish on the baking sheet and sprinkle generously with more salt to cover the fish entirely. Bake until done, about 12 minutes to the inch of thickness (including the salt crust), 25 to 30 minutes. Remove from the oven and let cool slightly on a rack.

Crack the salt layer with a knife. The skin and salt crust should be easily removed to expose 2 fillets that will have separated from the spine during cooking. Gently remove the fillets with a knife. Remove the spine and repeat the procedure for the remaining 2 fillets.

Serves 4

THE UPPER CRUST
Enclosing fish fillets in a moisture-retaining crust has the added benefit of creating a thicker piece of fish that requires somewhat less precision to cook; there will be less chance of overcooking. Potatoes make an especially nice edible crust, whether sliced paper thin and wrapped around a fillet, or mashed and spiked with herbs or grated horseradish. Other edible crusts to improvise: zucchini slices, mustard, or fresh tomato.

SALMON WITH MUSTARD

This perfumy delicious fish is moist and makes a nice light, easy dinner that is deceptively simple. Fish can easily dry out under the broiler; this recipe seals in the juices with a layer of mustard. Serve with a blanched green vegetable and simple boiled potatoes.

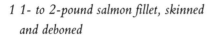

1 1- to 2-pound salmon fillet, skinned and deboned	Freshly ground black pepper
Salt	½ cup Dijon mustard
	¼ cup heavy cream

Preheat the broiler. Adjust the rack so that it is 4 to 5 inches from the heat source.

Place the fillet in a roasting pan. Season the fillet with salt and pepper. In a small bowl, combine the mustard and heavy cream. Spread the mixture evenly over the top of the fish, place under the broiler, and cook 8 to 10 minutes per inch of thickness. Remove from the oven and cut into serving portions.

Serves 4 to 6

Variation: Instead of the mustard and cream, sprinkle the salmon with 1 tablespoon chopped fresh basil and 1 tablespoon chopped fresh parsley. Cover the fish with ¼-inch-thick slices of tomato, leaving no flesh exposed. Season with salt and pepper.

ORIENTAL BAKED SALMON

The Oriental flavors come up from behind to envelop this fish, yielding a full rich taste with a hint of spice. It is a matter of debate in my house about whether to serve the salmon in fillets or steaks. The boneless fillet is more elegant, but the steaks are more compact. The difference in cooking times is negligible, so suit your own fancy! Serve on a bed of spinach or with snow peas.

1 tablespoon vegetable oil

1 medium onion, sliced

1 to 1½ pounds salmon fillet or
  1-inch-thick steaks

½ tablespoon Oriental sesame oil

3 tablespoons soy sauce

1 tablespoon water

1 teaspoon brown sugar (optional)

2 tablespoons dry sherry (optional)

¼ teaspoon Tabasco sauce

1 teaspoon finely chopped fresh ginger

Salt

Freshly ground black pepper

FOLDING FISH

Fish fillets such as flounder and sole may be folded in half or in thirds, to make a thicker fillet if it is so thin it runs the risk of being dry or unattractive when cooked. When using skinless fillets, put the skin side inside; if the skin has not been removed, keep the skin side outside. Fold the fillets in thirds like a business letter, or fold the two ends toward the middle if that is easier.

Preheat the oven to 400°F. Grease a large ovenproof dish.

Heat the oil in a small pan over medium heat. Add the onion and sauté until soft, about 5 minutes.

Transfer the onion to the ovenproof dish, and top with the fish fillet.

In a small mixing bowl, combine the sesame oil, soy sauce, water, brown sugar if using, sherry if using, Tabasco, and ginger. Pour this mixture over the fish, and sprinkle with salt and pepper. Cover the baking dish tightly with aluminum foil. Bake 12 to 15 minutes or until just done—the salmon will be opaque but will not look dry.

Serves 4

EIGHTEEN-MINUTE HERBED SCALLOPS

For entertaining, I like a dish that can be assembled in advance, since this leaves me with fewer dirty pans in the sink. Yet I love a lot of flurry at the table and want people to ooh and aah because the meal is so pretty. This recipe fills the bill perfectly. You'll use it over and over, as I do!

2 pounds Italian plum tomatoes, peeled, seeded, and chopped
2 tablespoons chopped fresh parsley
2 teaspoons chopped fresh basil leaves
1 garlic clove, peeled and chopped
1 cup julienned or thickly grated zucchini
1 cup julienned peeled carrot
1 cup white part of leek, well washed and julienned
1 pound sea scallops, patted dry
Salt
Freshly ground black pepper
Fresh lemon juice

Preheat the oven to 450°F. Place 4 pieces of aluminum foil or parchment paper on a baking sheet.

In a bowl, combine the tomatoes, parsley, basil, and garlic. In another bowl, combine the zucchini, carrot, and leek. Divide half of the zucchini mixture among the 4 pieces of aluminum foil or parchment paper, then top with half of the tomato mixture divided among the 4 portions. Arrange the scallops on top of the tomatoes, season with salt and pepper, and sprinkle with lemon juice. Layer the remaining vegetables over the scallops and top with the remaining tomato mixture. Cover with another piece of foil or parchment and fold the edges together to seal the packets. May be assembled to this point up to 4 hours in advance.

Place the packets on a baking sheet and bake 18 minutes. Transfer the unopened packets to dinner plates and let your guests open them at the table—but warn them about the burst of steam.

Serves 4

Beautiful Shrimp or Scallop Stir-Fry

Gloriously beautiful, fresh tasting, and easy, this dish is perfect for entertaining as well as for family meals. My grocery store has spinach that's prewashed—all it needs is a rinse and a shake and it's ready to use. I add pasta or rice to the meal to finish it off.

1½ cups fresh spinach, largest stems removed

2 red bell peppers, seeded and cut in 1-inch strips

2 yellow bell peppers, seeded and cut in 1-inch strips

10 leaves fresh basil

2 tablespoons soy sauce

2 tablespoons rice wine vinegar

1 tablespoon peeled and finely chopped garlic

1 teaspoon red pepper flakes

1 tablespoon Oriental sesame oil

3 tablespoons peanut oil

1 pound large shrimp, peeled and deveined, or sea scallops

Salt

Freshly ground black pepper

Wash the spinach and shake off some of the excess water. Heat a very large frying pan over medium-high heat. Add the spinach and sauté, stirring, until cooked, 3 to 5 minutes. Remove the spinach to a warmed bowl or platter and set aside.

In a medium bowl, combine the pepper strips, basil leaves, soy sauce, vinegar, garlic, and red pepper flakes.

Heat the sesame and peanut oils in a large frying pan or wok over medium-high heat. Add the pepper mixture and cook, tossing and stirring, for 3 to 5 minutes. Add the seafood and cook until done, 3 to 5 minutes longer. Season to taste with salt and pepper. Serve on a bed of the lightly wilted spinach.

Serves 4

SPINACH SUBSTITUTES
Lots of interesting greens are sold nationally and would make an interesting substitute for spinach. Mizuna, broccoli rape, or dandelions would be delicious—and some stores now carry a "braising mix" similar to the spring mix of tender greens for salad but that takes well to wilting and stir-frying. The mix usually includes mustards, chard, arugula, mizuna, even baby beet greens, which are so flavorful.

Sesame-Ginger Fried Shrimp

KITCHEN EQUIPMENT
Choosing the proper cookware is especially important to the time-pressured cook. Use nonstick electric frying pans and steamers to reduce cleanup time. Good heavy saucepans and pots help avoid scorching sauces and having to redo them.

These crispy, savory bites make a delicious starter or finger food, but they are particularly welcome when served as a main course. The shrimp fry fast, so watch them carefully, taking extra care not to let the sesame seeds burn. Everything else for dinner should be ready to eat and kept warm when you start to heat the oil. Your batter ingredients should be measured and organized so you can pay attention to the frying, and so you don't have to juggle other pans at the same time. A salad, rice, and sautéed snow peas would make for a fabulous, fast meal. Serve hot or at room temperature.

Oil for frying

1 tablespoon soy sauce

2 teaspoons sesame oil

½ cup milk, plus an additional 1 to 2 tablespoons if needed

1 egg

½ cup flour

¼ cup cornmeal

2 tablespoons sesame seeds

1 teaspoon ground ginger

2 pounds medium or large shrimp, peeled and deveined

Fill a cast-iron skillet no more than half full of oil and heat to 350° F. Meanwhile, in a medium bowl combine the soy sauce, sesame oil, milk, egg, flour, cornmeal, sesame seeds, and ginger. Add another tablespoon or so of milk, if needed, to make a nice thin batter. Using tongs, dip the shrimp in the batter, then place them immediately in the hot oil, working in batches if necessary. (The oil should cover the shrimp.) Fry until done, about 2 to 3 minutes, turning once. Remove and drain on paper towels. Keep warm in a 200° F. oven while frying the remaining shrimp. Serve hot.

Serves 4 to 6

BROILED SCALLOPS WITH PARMESAN

Although I love this dish with Parmigiano-Reggiano, I have substituted Fontina with a good result. I serve something green—snow peas or broccoli are my two favorites—for color contrast on the plate.

1 pound sea scallops
½ cup dry white wine or fresh lemon
 juice
1 to 2 teaspoons olive oil
3 tablespoons grated imprted Parmesan
 cheese

Salt
Freshly ground black pepper
1 teaspoon finely chopped fresh oregano,
 marjoram, or basil (optional)

Preheat the broiler.

Rinse the scallops and pat them dry. In a mixing bowl, whisk together the wine or lemon juice, oil, 2 tablespoons of the Parmesan, and salt and pepper to taste. Add the scallops and stir to coat. Spread the scallops on a baking sheet and sprinkle with the rest of the Parmesan. Place the baking sheet about 6 inches from the heat and broil until browned, about 2 minutes. Transfer to a serving bowl and sprinkle with the herbs, if using.

Serves 4

PATTI'S TROUT WITH PISTACHIO CRUST

Although fish doesn't usually lend itself to advance cooking, this dish can be breaded ahead of time and left in the refrigerator up to 24 hours, making it a truly last-minute affair that can be on the table 15 minutes after you walk in the door. The cooked dish also reheats very well in a conventional oven for 5 to 10 minutes at 350°F.

1½ cups pistachio nuts, very finely chopped with 2 tablespoons flour
½ cup fine, dry breadcrumbs
1 tablespoon grated lemon peel (no white attached)
2 teaspoons chopped fresh rosemary

Salt
Freshly ground black pepper
4 6-ounce trout fillets
2 egg whites beaten with 1 tablespoon water
Lemon wedges

Preheat the oven to 400°F.

In a large bowl, mix together the pistachio nuts, breadcrumbs, lemon peel, rosemary, and salt and pepper to taste. Pat the fillets dry with a paper towel. Dip them into the egg white mixture, then into the pistachio crumbs, pressing lightly so they will adhere. May be done ahead to this point and refrigerated up to 24 hours. Place the fillets on a baking pan and cook 10 minutes per inch of thickness, including the coating, or until the fish is opaque. Serve at once with lemon wedges.

Serves 4

Uncle John's Ginger Tuna Steak

My friend John Markham likes spicy foods and fell in love with the hot soy sauce that is now available in many markets. (If you can't find it, use regular soy sauce with a dash of cayenne pepper.) It keeps this baked tuna dish incredibly moist. I prefer it, I think, to broiled or grilled tuna because there is less chance of it being overdone. This also makes for outstanding leftovers; John's been known to cook a half-pound tuna steak, seasoned as below, and serve half the fish one evening, hot with a pasta and green veggie. The next day he has the chilled leftover cooked tuna (redolent with ginger flavor) over salad greens with Caesar dressing. This is easily doubled for four.

1 ¾ to 1 pound fresh tuna steaks, 1
   inch thick
1 teaspoon olive oil
1 tablespoon chopped fresh ginger

¼ cup hot soy sauce or soy sauce plus
   cayenne pepper to taste
¼ cup white wine or fresh or canned
   chicken stock or broth

Preheat the oven to 400°F.

Pat the tuna steaks dry, and then sprinkle both sides lightly with olive oil. Mix the ginger, hot soy sauce, and wine. Pour some of the mixture into a shallow glass or enamel baking pan, lay the tuna steak in the pan, and pour on the remaining sauce mixture. Bake, uncovered, 10 minutes. The thickness of the steaks varies, so cook the fish 10 minutes per inch of thickness; tuna will be cooked through in this amount of baking time. If there is tough skin, remove it. Serve with a light pasta and green vegetable side dish.

Serves 2

LEFTOVER TUNA

For an entrée salad, cook the tuna several hours ahead. Allow it to cool to room temperature, covered. It can show up again in several ways: You can toss it into a Caesar salad, add the pieces to a Salade Niçoise, toss with hot cooked pasta or cold pasta salad, or mince it and turn it into burgers. Also tuck cooked tuna into tacos with green sauce, olives, and lettuce.

CHICKEN BREASTS WITH APPLES AND CHEESE

CHICKEN BREASTS

Chicken breasts vary widely in size and nomenclature. They may either be the whole chest, also called whole breasts, or the split chest, also called split breasts. When they are sold in large family packs, with the bone in, they tend to be larger than those sold boned as cutlets, which are usually smaller whole breasts, boned, including the tenders. Choose the size that is appropriate for your recipe; I find the larger breasts make a more satisfying serving if they are to be cooked whole, but the smaller ones are great for stir-fries, slicing into salads, or grilling on skewers.

The tart flavor of Granny Smith apples boosts the pleasure quotient of this dish, which is particularly nice when there's no time for languid conversation over cheese and apples before or after dinner. For the family I don't peel the apple, but I do for company. This recipe takes a little time in preparation but is well worth the effort. The sauce is really rich and splendid.

4 boneless, skinless chicken breasts
1 Granny Smith apple, thinly sliced
4 slices white cheddar or Gouda
½ cup flour
Salt
Freshly ground black pepper
2 tablespoons (¼ stick) butter

1 small onion, finely chopped
Sprig of fresh thyme
1 bay leaf
1 cup apple juice
1 cup fresh or canned chicken stock or
  broth
½ tablespoon cornstarch

Butterfly the chicken by slicing each breast almost in half horizontally and opening outward like a book. Place 2 thin slices of apple on the lower half of each breast. Top with a slice of cheese and cover with the top half of breast.

Combine the flour, salt, and pepper on wax paper. Dredge the chicken breasts in the seasoned flour; shake off the excess. Heat 1 tablespoon of the butter in a large skillet. Add the chicken and cook 3 to 5 minutes on each side just until opaque throughout. Keep warm.

Heat the remaining tablespoon of butter in the same skillet over medium heat. Add the onion, thyme, and bay leaf and cook until the onion is soft and translucent, about 3 to 5 minutes. Add the apple juice and stir to scrape up the browned bits. Reduce the sauce by half over medium-high heat, about 5 minutes. Combine the chicken stock and cornstarch. Whisk into the reduced apple juice, bring to the boil, and simmer about 2 minutes or until thickened. Pass the sauce separately.

Serves 4

BASIC GRILLED OR BROILED CHICKEN BREASTS

This is my basic recipe for grilling chicken breasts, as well as other thin meats and poultry. It's an indispensable building block for fast meals with endless uses. Serve warm with your favorite chutney or salsa on the side, on a bed of vegetables, topped with a sauce, accompanied by couscous with peppers, or sliced and at room temperature in a salad. Be sure everything else is ready to serve once you start the chicken, as it cooks in no time.

4 boneless, skinless chicken breasts
1 tablespoon olive oil
1 tablespoon fresh lemon juice

1 tablespoon ground cumin, curry, ginger, or fresh chopped herbs (optional)
Salt
Freshly ground black pepper

Preheat the grill or broiler.

Place the chicken breasts in a shallow dish. In a small bowl combine the olive oil, lemon juice, seasoning if desired, and salt and pepper to taste. Pour over the chicken breasts and turn to coat well on both sides.

Place the chicken breasts on the hot grill or on a pan under the broiler, and cook 3 to 5 minutes per side, depending on the size, until just opaque throughout. Do not overcook or they will be tough.

Serves 4

BLACKBERRY CHICKEN

Necessity invented this dish when I wanted "something different" and had no time. It requires absolutely minimal preparation. The better the quality of the preserves you use, the nicer the final product. Make sure the breasts are evenly coated; the preserves make a nicely sweet yet slightly bitter crust.

4 chicken breasts, boned and skinned
1 cup blackberry preserves, beaten to
soften

Salt
Freshly ground black pepper

Preheat the broiler. Spray a roasting pan with nonstick spray. Place the rack 8 inches from the broiler.

Place the chicken breasts in a resealable plastic bag. Add the blackberry preserves. Season with salt and pepper. Coat the chicken, remove, and place the chicken in the roasting pan. Broil 8 minutes on each side, or until cooked through and nicely crusted.

Serves 4

SALSA CHICKEN

CHICKEN TENDERS
The tender, or tenderloin, is the long, thin piece of meat attached to the breast by a membrane next to the rib. I usually remove the tender when I'm cooking breasts as it gives thickness to the cutlet and add them to a container in the freezer. When I've stockpiled enough for a meal, I use them to make wonderful stir-fries. Chicken tenders are sold in bulk as well and are ideal for kebabs and other quick dishes. Kids really like them grilled or fried—a healthy homemade alternative to fast food!

Sometimes the easiest meal is one that can be assembled quickly and left to cook with no attention. With this recipe you have the option of putting it together at the last minute as well as making it ahead and reheating, as it becomes more tender and moist after a day. I use a homemade or commercial salsa, depending on my time. If cilantro is not available, you can create an entirely different flavor by substituting fresh basil.

4 boneless, skinless chicken breasts
Salt
Freshly ground black pepper

1 cup Tomato Salsa (page 28)
1 cup grated Monterey Jack cheese
2 tablespoons chopped fresh cilantro

Preheat the oven to 350°F.

Place the chicken breasts in a 9 × 13-inch baking dish. Season both sides with salt and pepper. Pour the salsa over the chicken. Bake 25 minutes. Remove from the oven. Change the oven setting to broil. Top the chicken with the cheese and cook until bubbly and light golden brown, about 3 minutes. Just before serving, sprinkle with the cilantro.

Serves 4

ROASTER BREAST WITH CRANBERRY RELISH

Like a mini-Thanksgiving dinner that's ready in a fraction of the time, a roaster breast gets a festive lift from a simple cranberry relish. Since cranberries freeze so well, it is no problem to have them on hand year round. I was particularly delighted with this very typical relish when French visitors oohed and aahed about it! You'll have extra relish, which can be refrigerated up to 3 days, frozen, or put in jelly jars and canned in a boiling water bath 15 minutes. Serve the traditional way with turkey or other poultry, or, in the summer, simmer a jar of it with blueberries and a little cinnamon and serve over hot biscuits.

1 2½-pound whole roasting chicken
    breast
1 tablespoon olive oil
Salt
Freshly ground black pepper

RELISH
1 cup sugar
1 cup water
Chopped peel (no white attached) of 1
    orange
1 12-ounce package fresh or defrosted
    cranberries

ROASTER PARTS
In many parts of the country it is possible to buy just the breast or thighs of roasting chickens—those weighing 4½ to 6½ pounds. While not as meaty as a turkey breast, a roaster breast will feed 3 to 4 handily and cooks in less time. Don't confuse them with broiler/ fryer breasts, which run 1 to 1½ pounds.

Preheat the oven to 425°F.

Rub the roaster breast with the oil and season with salt and pepper. Place in a baking dish and roast for 20 minutes; reduce the heat to 350°F and roast 20 minutes longer or until it reaches an internal temperature of 175°F.

While the breast roasts (or well in advance), combine the sugar and water in a 1-quart saucepan and bring to the boil. Add the orange peel and cranberries, return to the boil, reduce heat, and simmer 15 minutes. Remove from the heat. When the breast is done, transfer to a cutting board and allow to rest for 10 minutes. Slice thinly and serve with relish.

Serves 4

TARRAGON CHICKEN

DEGLAZING DEMYSTIFIED

Deglazing a pan creates a tasty sauce of cooking juices that can be served with the meat as is, or combined with a little cream, lemon juice, and spices to make a true gravy. This type of "quick" sauce adds depth of flavor to meats and may be poured over side dishes of rice or potatoes as well.

To deglaze your pan, add about a cup of liquid such as stock or wine to a pan in which meat has been browned (water will work, but doesn't add any flavor). Heat the pan of liquid over a burner and scrape a spoon (wooden works best) around the pan to loosen the fat and juices that have dried along the sides. To intensify the sauce, boil the original liquid down and add another cup or so of extra wine. All of the goodness from the pan will come together and thicken up as the liquid evaporates.

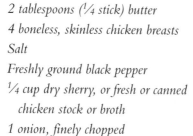

A double shot of tarragon gives this homey chicken recipe a flavor that brings to mind the fare of my favorite little Parisian bistro. Tarragon can vary widely, so always start with less than the recommended amount and add more to taste. Serve it with rice pilaf and a simple vegetable to accent the tarragon. Substitute 1 cup canned stewed tomatoes for the fresh tomatoes if they are out of season. And, if you need to vary even more, use basil or thyme.

2 tablespoons (¼ stick) butter
4 boneless, skinless chicken breasts
Salt
Freshly ground black pepper
¼ cup dry sherry, or fresh or canned chicken stock or broth
1 onion, finely chopped

1 medium tomato, peeled, cored, seeded, and chopped
½ cup tarragon vinegar
2 tablespoons chopped fresh tarragon or 2 teaspoons dried
Sugar (optional)

In a large ovenproof skillet, heat 1 tablespoon of the butter over high heat. Pat the breasts dry, season with salt and pepper, and cook quickly on both sides until golden brown and nearly cooked through, about 2 minutes per side. Remove the chicken and keep warm. Add the sherry to the skillet and stir over medium-high heat to deglaze, scraping up the pan juices and bits in the skillet. Add the onion, tomato, and vinegar and cook 2 to 3 minutes. Stir in the remaining 1 tablespoon of butter. Return the breasts to the skillet, turn to coat with the sauce, and heat until cooked through, about 4 minutes. Stir in the tarragon one tablespoon at a time. Taste for seasoning, adding a bit of sugar if necessary, and serve immediately.

Serves 4

Turmeric Sesame Chicken

Sunny yellow in color, turmeric adds a touch that is as pleasing to the eye as it is to the palate. This quickly seared preparation is fast, delicious, and pretty; start it out over high heat, reducing the heat if the chicken begins to smoke. Serve with sautéed spinach or broccoli rabe.

½ cup sesame seeds
1 teaspoon ground ginger
1 teaspoon ground turmeric
4 boneless, skinless chicken breasts

Salt
Freshly ground black pepper
2 tablespoons vegetable oil

In a shallow bowl or pie plate, combine the sesame seeds, ginger, and turmeric. Pat the breasts dry with a paper towel and season with salt and pepper. Place the chicken in the sesame seed mixture and press to coat. Add the oil to a large skillet and heat on high. Add the breasts, skinned side down. Do not move or flip. Let cook, undisturbed, 3 to 5 minutes to seal and form a nice crust; then turn carefully and cook on the opposite side for 3 to 5 minutes or until done.

Serves 4

SIMPLE CASSEROLE CHICKEN

LEFTOVER LIFESAVERS

A well-seasoned sauce can unify and elevate even the motliest odds and ends, transforming them into an appealing one-dish meal. I've made a white sauce, added bits of sorry-looking cheese, poured it over a conglomeration of leftover cooked vegetables, cooked ham, chicken, etc., popped it in a casserole to bake and had a great meal. Topping it with some buttered bread crumbs usually makes it more magical.

Leftover beef—whether broken-up cooked hamburgers or cooked steak—particularly loves a tomato sauce. Slice up cooked beef and add warm tomato sauce flavored with fresh herbs and maybe a little cooked onion. It's great over pasta, rice, or potatoes or just by itself! Top with cheese and run in the hot oven or under the broiler and you have a winner.

What an unglamorous name for a glorious dish! Casserole cooking is a technique that has fallen from favor in recent years but is particularly well suited to chicken. I return to this preparation over and over, adding ingredients to it, depending on the whim of the day and the purchases of my last shopping trip. The trick to it all is the pan. A heavy casserole that can take heat on the range top is the secret, though a nonstick pan may be used if heavy enough.

There are no hard and fast rules governing this recipe. Sometimes I allow the chicken to brown in the butter—through design or carelessness—which gives it a nutty flavor. Other times I add carrots, mushrooms and/or onions, and cook them until they are tender, and add the partially cooked chicken on top, to continue cooking another 10 minutes. Ribbons of zucchini or a few handfuls of spinach can be added at the end. Whipping cream added to the pan juices and boiled down until thick and lustrous makes it terribly elegant; chicken broth, reduced until thick, adds another dimension. And a squeeze of lemon never hurt anything! Let your conscience be your guide. Accompaniments should include rice and a green vegetable if one is not incorporated into the dish.

2 tablespoons oil or butter	Salt
4 boneless, skinless chicken breasts	Freshly ground black pepper
2 tablespoons chopped fresh herbs, such as parsley, thyme, tarragon, and/or oregano	

Heat a large heavy casserole with the oil or butter. When hot, add the chicken breasts in one layer and cook on one side until white. Turn. Add the fresh herbs, season to taste with salt and pepper, and cover. Reduce the heat to prevent burning and continue to cook on the stove top until the chicken bounces back when touched with a finger, 8 to 10 minutes. Serve warm directly from the pan, spooning the cooking juices over the chicken.

Serves 4

CHICKEN, TOMATO, AND VEGETABLE FRICASSEE

This one-dish meal is full of bright colors and delicious flavors, and its aroma wafting through the house never fails to bring questions of "What's for dinner?" It's great for company and quite special for a family supper, and needs no accompaniments, except perhaps dessert. It takes about 10 to 15 minutes to brown the chicken, time I use to get the slicing and chopping accomplished. But once it's all in the pan, there's nothing else to do. The saffron adds an enormous amount of flavor, but if it is too pricey for your budget it may be eliminated. Serve with a good bread to soak up the sauce.

3 tablespoons olive oil

1 3½-pound chicken, cut into serving pieces

4 cups thinly sliced onions and/or leeks, white part only, cut in 1-inch pieces

4 carrots, peeled and shredded

6 garlic cloves, peeled and chopped

1 28-ounce can plum tomatoes, drained and coarsely chopped

1 tablespoon fennel seeds

2 teaspoons dried or fresh thyme leaves

½ teaspoon saffron (optional)

2 bay leaves, crumbled

½ teaspoon red pepper flakes

2 teaspoons grated orange peel (no white attached)

2 cups fresh or canned chicken stock or broth

Salt

Freshly ground black pepper

2 tablespoons coarsely chopped fresh parsley

In a large skillet or Dutch oven, heat the olive oil over medium heat. Add the chicken pieces and brown on both sides, about 5 minutes per side. Remove the chicken from the pan and add the onions or leeks, carrots, and garlic. Cook until soft, about 5 minutes. Stir in the tomatoes, fennel seeds, thyme leaves, saffron if using, bay leaves, red pepper flakes, orange peel, and chicken stock. Bring to the boil. Return the chicken pieces to the skillet, reduce the heat, cover, and cook until the chicken is tender, 30 to 35 minutes. Remove the lid and cook about 5 minutes longer, allowing some of the liquid to cook off. Season to taste with salt and pepper. Garnish with chopped parsley.

Serves 4 to 6

BROILED LEMON ROSEMARY CHICKEN

The first time I had chicken prepared this way was on a hotel terrace in a small town in Emilia-Romagna, Italy. We'd walked up and down the winding streets relishing its beauty and were ravenously hungry when we sat down, but the crisp-skinned, rosemary-perfumed chicken would have been marvelously memorable under any circumstances. The cooking method is simplicity itself, but this is a dish that really benefits from advance planning; if you've flattened and marinated the split birds in the morning there'll be nothing more to do at dinnertime than fire up the broiler or barbecue.

1 2-pound fryer or 2 Cornish hens, split up the backbone
Juice of 3 lemons
Chopped peel (no white attached) of 3 lemons

3 tablespoons finely chopped fresh rosemary
¼ cup olive oil
Salt
Freshly ground black pepper

Preheat the grill or broiler.

Flatten the chicken, place in a roasting pan, and pour the lemon juice over it. Put a heavy weight—such as a heavy pan or one weighted with cans—on top of the chicken. If possible, refrigerate several hours or even overnight. When ready to cook, remove the weight. Combine the lemon peel, rosemary, and olive oil and brush on the chicken. Season liberally with salt and pepper. Place the chicken skin side up on the grill or 7 inches from the broiler heat. Cook 25 minutes, turning as necessary, until a meat thermometer registers 170° F.

Serves 4

Variations: Rub the chicken with the grated peel (no white attached) of 3 oranges mixed with 1 tablespoon ground ginger, or a mixture of 1 teaspoon paprika, 1 teaspoon cumin, and 1 teaspoon ground coriander, and marinate and cook as above.

CHICKEN WITH RUTABAGA AND POTATOES

This spicy hot, sweet, savory dish is a tremendous hit in the wintertime when a dose of the islands is needed, and the longer it marinates, the zestier it will be. It makes me think of my wedding in Jamaica and less harried, more relaxed times. The rutabagas and golden potatoes are similar in flavor to a Caribbean yam but much more readily available. I chop the garlic, onions, and peppers in the food processor and leave them in when adding the rest of the sauce ingredients. If you're not pressed for time, for a completely different presentation you can roast the chicken whole; toss the vegetables with some of the reserved marinade and bake separately.

3 garlic cloves, peeled and chopped

1 cup chopped green onions (about 8)

2 jalapeño peppers, chopped (with their seeds)

3 tablespoons soy sauce

2 tablespoons lime juice

2 tablespoons lemon juice

1 tablespoon ground allspice

1 tablespoon dry mustard

1 tablespoon salt

1 tablespoon brown sugar

1 tablespoon chopped fresh thyme

1 3½-pound whole chicken, cut into 8 pieces

1 rutabaga, peeled and cut into 1-inch pieces

3 potatoes, cut into 1-inch pieces, preferably Yukon Gold

Salt

Freshly ground black pepper

1 cup fresh or canned chicken stock or broth or vermouth

Preheat the oven to 400° F. Lightly oil a 13 × 9 × 2-inch baking dish.

In a food processor or blender, mix together the garlic, green onions, jalapeño peppers, soy sauce, lime juice, lemon juice, allspice, mustard, salt, brown sugar, and thyme. Process until smooth.

Place the chicken pieces and the green onion marinade in a plastic resealable bag, turn to coat well, and marinate until ready to cook, up to 24 hours. Spread the rutabaga and potatoes in the prepared baking dish. Season to taste with salt and pepper. Add the chicken stock or vermouth. Remove the chicken from the marinade and place on top of the bed of vegetables. Roast 25 to 30 minutes or until the vegetables are tender and the chicken is cooked through.

Serves 4 to 6

CHICKEN WITH DRIED CHERRIES

Everything but the chicken can come from the pantry shelf for this over-the-top low-calorie dish. I frequently skin chicken thighs when I get them home from the grocery store and freeze them. But, even if I haven't had that foresight and am in a hurry, this is perfectly fine with the skin—it just increases the calorie quotient. The dish freezes well for up to 3 months.

1 tablespoon oil	*¼ cup dried cherries or cranberries*
3 to 4 pounds chicken thighs	*1 tablespoon sugar*
2 onions, cut into ½-inch cubes	*1 teaspoon dried oregano*
Juice of 1 lime or 1 lemon, or 1½ table-	*1 teaspoon dried thyme*
spoons red wine vinegar	*1 tablespoon Worcestershire sauce*
3 or 4 canned plum tomatoes, drained	*¼ cup dry vermouth*
and chopped	*2 cups cooked rice, couscous, or pasta*

Heat the oil in a Dutch oven or nonstick skillet over moderate heat. Add the chicken thighs and brown on one side, 4 to 5 minutes, then turn and brown on the other side. Remove the chicken and set aside. Drain off the excess fat, add the onions, and cook until soft, about 3 minutes. Return the chicken to the pan and add the lime juice, tomatoes, cherries, sugar, oregano, thyme, Worcestershire, and vermouth. Bring to the boil, reduce heat to low, cover, and simmer for 30 minutes. Serve with rice.

Serves 6 to 8

CHICKEN PROVENCE

I really like this no-fuss dish, which showcases the flavors of the South of France, especially if you use tiny Niçoise olives. (Warn your guests about the pits if you leave them in.) This dish reheats well.

3 slices bacon
½ onion, finely chopped
4 boneless, skinless chicken breasts
Salt
Freshly ground black pepper

2 tablespoons chopped fresh thyme or oregano leaves
⅓ cup small black olives, preferably pitted
4 zucchini, sliced on diagonal ⅛ inch thick

Preheat the oven to 350°F.

Slice the bacon crosswise into thin strips. Combine with the onion in a large skillet and cook over medium-high heat until the onion is soft, about 5 minutes. Pat the breasts dry and season with salt and pepper. Lightly brown the breasts on each side in the bacon-onion mixture. Add the thyme, black olives, and zucchini slices. Cover, reduce the heat, and cook until the chicken is done, 8 to 10 minutes. Serve hot.

Serves 4

THAI THIGHS

Delectable and very tangy, these spice-laden thighs are a good main course, as well as an incredible midnight snack that is low in fat, too! They may be cooked right away or marinated for a deeper, more pronounced flavor.

1¼ cups plain lowfat yogurt
2 teaspoons finely chopped fresh ginger
1½ teaspoons ground coriander
2 to 3 cloves garlic, peeled and finely chopped

Cayenne pepper to taste
¼ cup fresh lemon juice
Grated peel (no white attached) of 1 lemon
2 pounds chicken thighs

Preheat the oven to 350° F.

In a large mixing bowl or plastic bag, combine the yogurt, ginger, coriander, garlic, cayenne pepper, lemon juice, and peel. Add the chicken thighs and turn to coat well. Marinate while preheating the oven or up to 24 hours in the refrigerator.

When ready to cook, remove the chicken thighs from the marinade and place on a foil-lined baking sheet. Bake until cooked through, lightly brown, and bubbly, 25 to 30 minutes. Remove with a slotted spatula and discard juices and fat or use to season rice or couscous.

Serves 4 to 6

CORNISH HENS

Cornish hens are a pleasant alternative to chicken and a sensible choice for last-minute meals as they cook so quickly. Cutting and flattening the hens speeds up their already abbreviated cooking time even further. I find that one bird will usually feed two, even those with hearty appetites. You can adapt your favorite roast chicken seasonings. This recipe freezes and reheats well.

2 1½-pound Cornish hens
Grated peel (no white attached) of 3
  lemons
2½ tablespoons chopped fresh rosemary

Salt
Freshly ground black pepper
¼ cup vegetable oil

Place the Cornish hens on a cutting board, breast-side down. Split and butterfly the hens by cutting down the backbone, then crack the hen on either side of the backbone at the ribs by pressing down with the heel of your hand so that it will lie flat. Rub the hens with the lemon peel, rosemary, and salt and pepper to taste.

Heat the oil on medium-high heat in a large stovetop-proof roasting pan. Place the Cornish hens in the pan breast side down. Weight the hens down so that they will lie flat and cook evenly and faster. Cook, turning if necessary, until an instant-read thermometer reads 185° F., 8 to 10 minutes.

Serves 2 to 4

LEE ANNE'S SAVORY QUAIL

One of my apprentices devised this savory rub, which gives poultry a deep herb essence without marinating. It works exceptionally well with quail, which cooks up in less than 20 minutes and creates a perfectly elegant main course for 2. It would also make a lovely appetizer for 4 at a formal meal. Use a nonstick pan for easy cleanup.

QUAIL
These succulent little birds have come to be associated with very formal dining, which is a shame, because they are absolutely delicious, cook up quickly (even faster when split), and add an elegant fillip to everyday dinners. Quail are now farm raised (those I get come from South Carolina) and are widely available in the freezer case, where they generally come four to a package.

4 quail

1 tablespoon finely chopped fresh rosemary

1 tablespoon finely chopped fresh thyme

1½ teaspoons dried sage

2 tablespoons oil

Salt

Freshly ground black pepper

Cut the quail along the backbone. Turn the bird over and press on the breastbone to flatten it. Cut a slit into the skin on each breast.

Combine the rosemary, thyme, sage, and 1 tablespoon of the oil. Rub the birds with the mixture on the outer skin and in the slit. Season very well with salt and pepper.

Heat the remaining 1 tablespoon of oil in a large heavy nonstick skillet. Place the birds in the pan breast side down. Weight the birds down with another heavy skillet or pan. Cook on medium-high heat until they are a rich brown, 8 to 10 minutes. Turn the birds and cook until completely done and the juices run clear, another 5 to 8 minutes. Serve warm or at room temperature.

Serves 2

Tomato Lemon Beef with Gremolata ■ Untraditional Shish Kebabs ■
London Broil with Mushroom Dijon Gravy ■ Sautéed or Grilled Liver with
Onions ■ Beef Steaks with Herbs, Capers, and Spinach ■ Herb-Crusted
Tenderloin Steaks ■ Ribeye Steak with Oyster Sauce ■ Grilled Lamb Chops
with Herbed Garlic Paste ■ Veal Scallopini ■ Quick Finnish Leg of Lamb

THE MEAT LOCKER

■ Butterflied Leg of Lamb with Mint Pecan Pesto ■ Sausage and
Apples ■ Mediterranean Pork Chops ■ Very Orange Ginger Pork Chops ■
Flavorful Pork with Spinach and Soy Sauce ■ Grilled Mustard Pork
Chops ■ Five-Spice Pork Loin ■ Cranberry Tenderloin of Pork ■ Pork
and Onions with Pepper Jelly Sauce ■ Tomato Caper Pork Tenderloin

MEAT COOKS according to its thickness, not its weight. It follows, therefore, that thinly sliced, chopped, and cubed meats will cook faster than larger pieces.

When time is of the essence, the quickest thing to cook is butterflied or boneless pieces of meat and poultry, such as chicken breasts or boned leg of lamb, flank, sirloin, or tenderloin steak, and even thicker steaks or chops. Individual, smaller, thinner meats like scallopini are more difficult as they overcook easily and are labor intensive to make for a crowd, although of course, they are ready in just minutes. Sausage and hamburger meats are also much loved for their speed and ease of cooking.

Meats can't be separated from their sauces, marinades, and seasonings, for these are what give a dish its distinction. You can make a quick sauce for almost any meat from the juices released during cooking. Skim off the fat if necessary and, if the juices are scanty, add a hot liquid—broth, water, vinegar, fruit juice, or whipping cream. Then, scraping the pan, bring the sauce to the boil (called deglazing, see sidebar, page 77), and cook until somewhat reduced. Pour over the meat and serve.

Similarly, vinegars (particularly the exotic ones such as balsamic, raspberry, and sherry) and bottled sauces such as soy sauce and Worcestershire sauce make great instant sauces when a few simple ingredients are added—ginger, lemongrass, fresh herbs, or spices.

Tomato sauces and salsas are speedy too, and combine easily prepared ingredients for quick plate enhancers. Layering various flavors makes up for what is lost when slow cooking is not possible.

It is a big help to prepare meat when you come home from the grocery store. If possible, when freezing, freeze flat and separate, so that meats may be separated and defrosted individually to save time. If they are not already prepared by the butcher, remember half-frozen meat is easier to cut than flaccid, room temperature (or even cold-from-the-refrigerator) meat.

The methods of quick-cooking meats are endless and can easily be adapted to each other. You should consider the broiler and the grill interchangeable, although the former doesn't impart quite the same smoky flavor. A bit of oil or butter in a heavy skillet can usually stand in for either; a frying pan and wok can both do a stir-fry. A variety of techniques is important as otherwise foods taste like each other.

TOMATO LEMON BEEF WITH GREMOLATA

Gremolata, that delicious Italian blend of garlic, lemon, and parsley, gives simple roasted meat an air of distinction. Glamorous dishes like this one celebrate rather than disguise leftover meat, and are a good reason for cooking an extra roast to have in the freezer. Slice the meat before freezing and separate with sheets of plastic wrap or freezer paper so you can remove and thaw as much as needed. Ribeye steak works well in the lamb variation below.

LEFTOVER CASEROLES
Don't think of leftovers as second best—they are found gold for busy cooks. Even meats that might become dry if reheated will usually do well if reheated in a sauce or in a soup. Slice extra scallopini, ham, or roast beef into strips to change its personality. Make soups, stuff won ton or egg roll skins, and devise new salads or stir-fries to use up leftovers. And meats aren't the only leftovers that are good the second time around; add a bit of soy sauce or vinegar or dot with butter and fresh herbs to give a whole new twist to yesterday's vegetables.

1 pound cooked eye of round, chuck, sirloin tip, or other roast

¼ cup olive oil

1 large onion, sliced

2 garlic cloves, peeled and chopped

¾ pound Roma or cherry tomatoes, chopped roughly or 1 1-pound can Italian plum tomatoes, drained, juices reserved

1 teaspoon tomato paste

Grated peel (no white attached) of 1 lemon

2 tablespoons chopped fresh basil or dried to taste

Salt

Freshly ground pepper

Sugar

Divide the meat into four pieces, preferably thick slices. Heat the oil over medium-high heat in a heavy frying pan. Add the onion and half of the garlic and cook until soft, 4 to 5 minutes. Stir in the tomatoes, tomato paste, half the lemon peel, and the meat. Top with half the chopped basil and heat quickly. Season to taste with salt, pepper, and sugar. Remove the meat to a hot platter, stir the tomato mixture and pour over the meat. In a small bowl, mix together the remaining garlic, basil, and lemon peel and sprinkle over the meat.

Serves 4

Variation: Lamb with Tomato Gremolata Sauce: Season 4 5-ounce shoulder lamb chops or thick slices of leg of lamb with salt and pepper. Heat 2 tablespoons oil in a pan. Add the meat, brown on one side, turn, and brown on the second. Add the rest of the ingredients as above. Cook briefly and serve.

UNTRADITIONAL SHISH KEBABS

Either beef or lamb will work beautifully in this simple and colorful all-in-one dish. Almost any cut of boneless meat will do. The more tender, the better; leg of lamb or a sirloin, tenderloin, or rib roast of beef are all good candidates. The bulk of the work can be done ahead, making this a great company dish, and even if marinating and do-ahead fixing aren't possible, the kebabs are still delicious if they only marinate while you are cutting up the vegetables. The surprising seasoning blend breathes new life into a recipe that had come to seem a bit tired.

MARINADE
½ cup oil
½ cup apple cider vinegar
2 teaspoons dry mustard
2 to 4 tablespoons soy sauce
1 teaspoon dried thyme
2 teaspoons Worcestershire sauce
Salt
Freshly ground black pepper

2 pounds beef or lamb cut in 1- to 1½-inch cubes
2 medium tomatoes, cut in eighths, or 16 cherry tomatoes
1 small yellow squash, cut in 1-inch chunks
Spiced Couscous (page 150) or wild rice blend

Preheat the grill or broiler. If using wooden skewers, soak in water to prevent burning.

Mix together the oil, vinegar, dry mustard, soy sauce, thyme, and Worcestershire sauce. Season to taste with salt and pepper. Add the meat. Refrigerate, covered, as long as possible, 4 hours or up to overnight, turning occasionally. Remove the meat from the marinade and place on skewers, alternating with the tomato and squash.

Grill the skewers over medium-high heat on all sides for a total of 8 to 12 minutes, depending on the size of the meat chunks. Serve hot on a bed of Spiced Couscous or rice.

Serves 4

LONDON BROIL WITH MUSHROOM DIJON GRAVY

The large number of ingredients in this recipe belies the ease of its preparation, and it will appeal to both the traditionalists and the trendies at your table; fresh rosemary and horseradish give this a very contemporary flair. I season the meat and make the sauce up to 2 days ahead, so all I have to do at the last minute is cook the meat and reheat the sauce. Serve it rare, as this cut doesn't do as well when "well done." Use the time it takes to heat the grill or broiler to slice and chop, and then start the meat and the sauce simultaneously. (And don't forget to use the hot grill for something else when the meat is done—maybe charring a red pepper to be used another time.) The sauce is also good on just about any steak or chop. Leftovers are, of course, great for sandwiches.

LONDON BROIL
Many cuts of beef now go by the name of London broil; it traditionally referred to flank steak, but this lean cut has become so popular that the term is now applied to some cuts of round steak. I much prefer the flank steak for both texture and flavor.

1 1½-pound London broil or flank steak, about 2 inches thick
8 garlic cloves, peeled
2 tablespoons cracked pepper
2 tablespoons olive oil
2 tablespoons butter
1 onion, sliced
1½ cups mushrooms, sliced

1 tablespoon prepared horseradish
1 to 2 tablespoons chopped fresh rosemary
1 to 2 tablespoons Dijon mustard
1 tablespoon red wine vinegar
2 cups canned or fresh beef stock or broth
Salt
Freshly ground black pepper

Rub the meat with 2 of the garlic cloves, then press the pepper evenly on both sides. If possible, refrigerate for 3 hours or overnight.

Heat the olive oil and butter in a large pan until hot and singing. Chop the remaining 6 garlic cloves. Add the onion, mushrooms, remaining garlic, and horseradish and cook over medium heat until soft, about 5 minutes. Stir in the rosemary, mustard, vinegar, and beef stock, bring to the boil, then lower heat to a simmer, and reduce by half until the sauce is thick and creamy, about 5 to 10 minutes. Adjust seasonings with salt and pepper to taste. Tightly covered, the sauce can be refrigerated for several days.

Meanwhile, grill the meat over hot coals or broil 4 inches from the heat about 7 minutes per side or until a meat thermometer registers 140°F. for rare. Let the meat sit for 10 minutes, then slice thinly on the diagonal across the grain. Serve the meat with the warm sauce. Stir any accumulated juices into the warm sauce.

Serves 4 to 6

SAUTÉED OR GRILLED LIVER WITH ONIONS

ONION COMPOTE
Sautéed onions, cooked until their sugars caramelize and well seasoned, make an easy, delicious condiment for any rich meat, poultry, or fish that has been grilled or roasted. Add 2 to 3 tablespoons of balsamic or red wine vinegar to 2 large, sliced onions that have been sautéed in butter until soft. Boil down quickly until absorbed, and toss with 1 to 2 tablespoons mixed fresh herbs, such as basil, thyme, or parsley. The compote can be refrigerated for 3 or 4 days and reheated in the microwave.

Liver does equally well under the broiler, on the grill, or in the sauté pan, and no matter which method you choose it cooks in a trice. I lean toward the sauté pan since it can be used for the onions too. Liver doesn't really need a starch accompaniment; I prefer to serve it with several vegetables. Those who insist on a starch might be happy with a microwave "baked" potato or rice. For a slightly more elegant meal, top with an onion compote (see sidebar).

2 to 4 tablespoons butter
2 tablespoons oil

2 large onions, sliced thinly
1 pound calf's liver

In a large frying pan, heat 2 tablespoons of the butter and 1 tablespoon of the oil over medium heat. Add the onions and cook until a pale caramel brown. Remove the onions with a slotted spoon and set aside. Add the remaining butter if necessary and turn up the heat to medium high. Add the liver to the hot pan (alternately, heat the grill or broiler, brush the liver with the butter and oil from the pan). Cook 2 to 3 minutes per side for a deep brown exterior and a pink interior. Transfer to warmed plates and pile the cooked onions on top.

Serves 4

BEEF STEAKS WITH HERBS, CAPERS, AND SPINACH

A lusty red sauce and an abundant dose of garlic give this wonderful fall or winter all-in-one dish an Italian flair. I'm a lazy cook so I only use one pan, but if you want to speed up the cooking, get two pans going, one for the sauce and one for the meat; just be sure to add the sauce to the meat pan after all the meat has been sautéed to capture all those delicious juices! The butcher should be willing to pound the steaks for you. They cook so fast the onions, garlic, and red pepper really need to be sliced and the spinach defrosted before you get started. Then, while the sauce is cooking, chop the herbs and olives in batches in a mini food processor.

1/4 cup olive oil

4 4- to 6-ounce thin boneless sirloin
   steaks, pounded to 1/3-inch thickness

1 onion, sliced

1 red bell pepper, seeded and sliced

4 garlic cloves, peeled and chopped

1 16-ounce can whole peeled tomatoes
   with their juice, broken into large
   pieces

1 tablespoon red wine vinegar

1 12-ounce package frozen chopped
   spinach, defrosted and well drained

1 tablespoon chopped fresh or dried
   oregano

1 tablespoon chopped fresh or dried
   rosemary

Juice of 1 lemon

2 anchovy fillets, chopped

2 tablespoons capers, drained

1/2 cup chopped black olives (see Note)

Salt

Freshly ground black pepper

In a large skillet, heat the olive oil until very hot. Add the steaks and sauté quickly on very high heat, approximately 2 minutes per side. Set them aside on a plate and cover with foil to keep warm. Add the onion and bell pepper to the same pan, reduce the heat to medium, and cook until soft, about 10 minutes. Add the garlic, the tomatoes and their juice, and the wine vinegar and cook until thick and most of the liquid has cooked out, about 7 minutes. Add the drained spinach, oregano, rosemary, lemon juice, anchovies, capers, and olives.

Heat through, 2 to 3 minutes, and then return the meat to the pan. Cover and reheat quickly until the meat is hot. Season to taste with salt and pepper and serve at once.

Serves 4

NOTE: *To pit olives place a knife blade flat over them and smash with the heel of your hand; the olives will split, allowing the pit to be removed.*

HERB-CRUSTED TENDERLOIN STEAKS

BEEF TENDERLOIN
There is no more tender cut of beef than the tenderloin or filet mignon. It is also the most expensive, but it goes a long way and is certainly more economical than going out to eat. A tenderloin is good to roast whole if you have the time, but it is also great cut into steaks. Do not be fooled by cuts resembling the tenderloin. Quite often the eye of round, the least tender cut of beef, is packaged to resemble a filet steak. When in doubt, ask your butcher.

Fast-cooked food is particularly enhanced by the addition of fresh herbs, which give punch and a complexity of flavors; witness this aromatic topping for tender steaks. Serve with any of the traditional steak accompaniments—ribboned potatoes and green beans or broccoli are favorites—and don't forget the salad!

1 tablespoon chopped fresh thyme
1 tablespoon chopped fresh rosemary
1 tablespoon chopped fresh oregano
1 garlic clove, peeled and finely chopped
Salt

Freshly ground black pepper
4 tenderloin or filet mignon steaks, 1 to
1½ inches thick
1 tablespoon butter
1 tablespoon oil

In a small bowl, combine the thyme, rosemary, oregano, and garlic. Season to taste with salt and pepper. Rub the steaks on both sides with the herb mixture.

In a large skillet, heat the butter and oil over high heat. Add the steaks and cook 3 to 5 minutes. Turn the steaks and cook the other side for 3 to 5 minutes for rare steaks.

Serves 4

Ribeye Steak with Oyster Sauce

This piquant sauce accentuates the ribeye's dramatic flavor. Look for oyster sauce in the Oriental section of your grocery store. Distilled from oysters, its old-fashioned name is oyster ketchup. While the steaks cook, cut up some potatoes for a quick stir-fry or add them to the grill and make a green vegetable and salad while they are cooking, keeping an eye on the sauce.

3 tablespoons butter

2 medium onions, thinly sliced

$\frac{1}{3}$ cup oyster sauce

$\frac{1}{3}$ cup water

$\frac{1}{4}$ cup finely chopped fresh parsley

Freshly ground black pepper

4 8- to 10-ounce ribeye steaks, $\frac{3}{4}$ to 1 inch thick

Preheat the grill or broiler.

In a large skillet, melt the butter. Add the onions and cook over medium heat until soft, about 5 minutes. Pour in the oyster sauce and water and heat through. Add the parsley and pepper to taste. Set aside and keep warm until the steaks are done or make up to a day in advance and reheat.

Meanwhile, place the steaks on the hot grill, turning once, and grill them to the desired degree of doneness, about 5 minutes per side for rare, 7 minutes for medium, or 9 minutes for well done. Pour the sauce over the steaks and serve.

Serves 4

GRILLED LAMB CHOPS WITH HERBED GARLIC PASTE

MEDALLIONS
Medallions are round, individual portions that may be cut from fish, pork tenderloin, lamb, veal, beef tenderloin or ribs, or venison tenderloin or ribs. All may be treated essentially the same. They may be sautéed or grilled as is, or they may be flattened with a mallet or the flat side of a cleaver and quickly sautéed or grilled for a minute or so per side.

Either rib or loin chops are fine in this recipe, as are steaks cut from the leg. It's elegant, very easy, and pretty on the plate, and lamb is lower in cholesterol than many other meats. I like my lamb pink and juicy; cook it a minute or two longer than directed if you prefer well done.

2 garlic cloves, peeled
2 teaspoons kosher (coarse) salt
1 tablespoon chopped fresh rosemary
1 tablespoon chopped fresh thyme

2 to 3 tablespoons olive oil
6 to 8 lamb chops, 1½ inches thick
Freshly ground black pepper

Preheat the grill or broiler.

To make the garlic into a paste, place the garlic cloves and salt on a board and use a metal spatula to mash. Add the rosemary, thyme, and olive oil to the garlic.

Remove any fat from the chops. Spread the garlic paste on both sides of the lamb chops. Grill or broil them 5 to 6 minutes per side over medium-high heat, or until desired doneness is reached. Season to taste with pepper.

Serves 4

Veal Scallopini

Tender veal scallops, pounded paper thin, are menu staples in many fine French or Italian restaurants. They are so easy and quick to prepare, they should have a permanent place in your last-minute repertoire too. Fish fillets, turkey, pork, or chicken may easily be substituted for the veal and are often also called scallopini in the market. There are many options and variations on this dish; the simplest is just a squeeze of lemon juice.

¼ cup all-purpose flour
1 pound veal cutlets, pounded thin
  (about 4 to 6)
Salt
Freshly ground black pepper
2 tablespoons vegetable oil
4 tablespoons (½ stick) butter

Juice of 2 lemons
2 tablespoons chopped fresh parsley
  (optional)
2 tablespoons capers (optional)

GARNISH
1 lemon, sliced

Place the flour on a piece of wax paper or in a shallow dish. Season the veal with the salt and pepper. Dredge the veal scallopini in the flour and shake off any excess. In a skillet heat the oil and 2 tablespoons of the butter until sizzling hot. Add the veal (you may have to cook it in batches) and sauté on one side for 1 to 2 minutes or until browned. Turn and brown on the second side. Remove from the pan and keep warm on a serving platter. Repeat until all the meat is browned. Add the rest of the butter to the pan and cook over medium heat until it just begins to brown. Remove the pan from the heat and add the lemon juice, parsley, and capers if using. Pour over the veal. Garnish with the lemon slices and serve immediately.

Serves 4

QUICK FINNISH LEG OF LAMB

When I visited the Arctic Circle in Finland, I was served a meal prepared by a reindeer farmer. He cooked it in a pan over an open wood fire, slicing pieces of frozen leg of reindeer directly into sizzling fat in the pan. A little salt and pepper and a cranberry or other tart jelly (he used loganberry) finished it off. It was delicious!

I doubt that I'll ever get reindeer again; so I decided to try the technique with lamb and it is just as tasty. Obviously, this recipe multiplies up and you can use the whole leg if you need to serve a crowd in a hurry. The frozen meat slices surprisingly easily; if it is frozen too hard to slice, a few minutes on the counter or in the microwave should get it just right. Use what you need and return the rest to the freezer.

¼ to ½ cup (½ to 1 stick) butter
¼ to ½ cup oil
1 frozen leg of lamb or 1½ pounds leg
* of lamb meat, frozen*

Salt
Freshly ground black pepper
1 cup loganberry or cranberry sauce or
* jelly*

Heat enough of the butter and oil to cover the bottom of a large frying pan. With a very sharp knife, cut thin (⅛- to ¼-inch-thick) slices of the lamb into the sizzling fat. Brown and turn. Brown the second side quickly. Keep warm while cooking additional slices of lamb. Season to taste with salt and pepper and serve immediately with the sauce or jelly. Return any unused lamb to the freezer.

Serves 4

Variation: Try farm-raised venison, or white-tail, if you have a hunter in the family.

BUTTERFLIED LEG OF LAMB WITH MINT PECAN PESTO

Boneless leg of lamb is ideal for a dinner party because its uneven thickness gives your guests a choice of rare, medium, or well-done meat, and it cooks in less than half an hour. The marinade can be heated with the juice from the carving platter and poured over the sliced lamb. The "pesto," made from mint and pecans rather than the traditional basil and pine nuts, can be made several days ahead and kept refrigerated or frozen, where it will keep for 2 months. Present the meat on a pretty platter and slice with ease and a flourish in front of your guests. It may be made ahead and reheated, or served cold.

MARINADE

½ cup olive oil

2 tablespoons red wine vinegar

2 tablespoons chopped fresh rosemary

2 tablespoons chopped fresh oregano

2 tablespoons chopped fresh lemon peel
 (no white attached) or lemon balm
 (optional)

4 garlic cloves, peeled and chopped

1 5- to 6-pound leg of lamb, butterflied,
 and trimmed of all visible fat and
 membranes

MINT PESTO

2 cups fresh mint leaves, packed (or half
 parsley)

4 garlic cloves, peeled

½ cup pecans

¾ cup grated imported Parmesan cheese

½ to ¾ cup olive oil

In a large bowl, combine the olive oil, vinegar, rosemary, oregano, lemon peel if using, and garlic. Cut a series of small incisions in the lamb. Place in the bowl and rub on all sides with the marinade. Place in a covered bowl or resealable bag and marinate overnight, if possible, in the refrigerator.

Prepare the grill or place a rack 5 inches under the preheated broiler. Remove the meat from the marinade. Cook about 15 minutes per side, or until a meat thermometer registers 140°F. in the thickest portion. Let the lamb rest 10 minutes before carving.

Meanwhile, prepare the pesto. In a food processor or blender, combine the mint leaves, garlic cloves, pecans, and Parmesan cheese and process until finely chopped. With the machine running, add the olive oil in a slow, steady stream until a thick sauce forms.

Slice the lamb on the diagonal and arrange on a platter. Pass the pesto separately.

Serves 8 to 10

SAUSAGE AND APPLES

I love the spicy-sweet combination of pork and apples. This recipe multiplies easily and reheats very well. It is equally at home for breakfast, brunch, or a fall or winter supper, served over soft polenta.

1 pound bulk pork sausage

4 Granny Smith apples, cored and cut into ½-inch chunks

½ teaspoon caraway seeds, crushed

1 tablespoon finely chopped fresh parsley

1 tablespoon finely chopped fresh sage

Salt

Freshly ground black pepper

Brown the sausage in a large skillet over medium-high heat, breaking it up as it browns. Push the cooked meat to one side of the skillet and add the apple pieces. Cook 3 to 4 minutes, stirring occasionally. Stir in the caraway seeds, parsley, and sage and heat through. Season to taste with the salt and pepper and serve hot.

Serves 4

MEDITERRANEAN PORK CHOPS

These chops with their combination of Mediterranean ingredients are good with couscous or a larger pasta.

8 to 10 boneless loin chops, ½ inch
   thick (2 to 2½ pounds)
Salt
Freshly ground black pepper
1 10¾-ounce can tomato purée

1 tablespoon capers, chopped
1 tablespoon chopped anchovies
1 tablespoon finely chopped fresh
   rosemary

Preheat the broiler. Spray a large baking sheet with nonstick spray.

Season both sides of the chops with salt and pepper. In a resealable plastic bag, place the chops, tomato purée, capers, anchovies, and rosemary. Let marinate at least 20 minutes or overnight, if possible.

Place the coated chops on the baking sheet. Broil 4 to 5 inches from the heat until juicy and barely pink in the center, 3 to 4 minutes per side.

Serves 6 to 8

VERY ORANGE GINGER PORK CHOPS

The name says it all—orange dominates these lovely chops. Again, marinating in the refrigerator works to flavor the meat while you do other things. Try to get them in the fridge in the morning for a flavorful entrée that cooks in less than 10 minutes.

1 cup orange juice
Finely chopped peel (no white attached)
   of 2 oranges
1 garlic clove, peeled and finely chopped
3 tablespoons finely chopped fresh ginger
1 tablespoon red pepper flakes (optional)

1 tablespoon vegetable oil
6 to 8 pork chops, preferably ½-inch
   boneless loin chops (1½ to 2 pounds)
Salt
Freshly ground black pepper

PORK CHOPS
Pork chops are available from grocery stores and meat counters in various types and sizes. Almost all are tender. Choose chops that have a high proportion of meat to fat and bone.

One center-cut ½-inch loin chop with bone in weighs approximately 5 ounces. A package of those chops weighing 2 or 2½ pounds would contain 6 to 8 chops.

One boneless loin chop ½ inch thick weighs approximately 4 ounces. A package of those chops weighing 1½ to 2 pounds would contain 6 to 8 chops.

("Breakfast" chops are a thinner loin cut and cook in 3 to 5 minutes TOTAL and are not specified here, but they may be used if time is adjusted to prevent overcooking.)

There is little difference in the time it takes to cook bone-in or bone-out—it is the thickness that matters.

Preheat the broiler. Line a baking sheet with foil and grease it.

In a resealable plastic bag, combine the orange juice, peel, garlic, ginger, red pepper flakes, and oil. Add the pork chops and marinate at least 1 hour or overnight, if possible, in the refrigerator. Remove the pork chops from the marinade. Season each side with salt and pepper. Place on the prepared baking sheet and broil 4 to 5 inches away from the heat for 3 to 5 minutes on each side, depending on thickness.

Serves 4 to 6

FLAVORFUL PORK WITH SPINACH AND SOY SAUCE

GROUND MEAT
Because small pieces of meat will always cook faster than large ones, ground meats should have a home in any quick meal repertoire. And don't stop with beef: ground veal, pork, chicken, and turkey are all inexpensive and versatile. A base of ground meat, onion, and garlic can be enhanced many ways: add beans and seasonings for a fast chili, form into meatballs and sauté, stuff into dumpling wrappers and steam, or shape around a skewer and grill. Any of these preparations should be ready to eat in under thirty minutes.

Frozen spinach is an absolute must in any freezer. It's a timesaver adaptable to many different cooking methods, and this dish is a perfect example. Here it's combined with fast-cooking ground pork and Asian flavorings.

1 pound ground pork or beef or a mixture
1 onion or 5 green onions, chopped
2 garlic cloves, peeled and chopped
¼ to ½ cup sherry
½ cup soy sauce

1 teaspoon anise seeds, ground star anise, or ground anise seed
1 10-ounce package frozen whole-leaf spinach, thawed and pressed to remove liquid
3 cups cooked pasta, drained

Heat a large frying pan. Add the pork, onion, and garlic and cook until light brown and thoroughly cooked, about 5 minutes, breaking up the meat and turning it as it cooks. Drain any fat. Add the sherry, soy sauce, and anise seeds to the pork and toss to mix well. Add the spinach and pasta, cover, and heat about 5 minutes. Toss and serve hot.

Serves 4

GRILLED MUSTARD PORK CHOPS

I find mustard and pork are natural partners. There is nothing of the ballpark in this, however. The dish is fit for an elegant evening when accompanied by artichoke hearts or green peas or served on a hot summer's night with a cold ratatouille. This is great for a meal when you don't have any time to fix ahead. It's easy to throw on the grill for a weeknight supper. The semi-charred pork is especially memorable. I find chops are particularly satisfying—they make you feel fed. Any pork chop will do, should you not have just the type specified below.

½ cup Dijon mustard

2 tablespoons olive oil

2 teaspoons Worcestershire sauce

2 teaspoons dried rosemary

½ to 1 teaspoon ground cumin or
coriander (optional)

Salt

Freshly ground black pepper

8 to 12 center-cut boneless pork loin
chops, ½ inch thick (2 to 2¾
pounds)

Spray the grill with nonstick spray. Preheat the broiler or grill.

In a small mixing bowl or measuring cup, combine the mustard, olive oil, Worcestershire, rosemary, cumin if desired, and salt and pepper to taste.

Brush the chops on both sides with the mustard mixture and grill or broil 3 to 4 minutes per side, until bubbly with a few dark brown spots. Serve hot or at room temperature.

Serves 6 to 8

GRILLING

Grilling is a general catch-all word for searing quickly on a hot surface. But hectic schedules don't always have room for firing up the charcoal in an outdoor barbecue. To get that same char-grilled taste I use a number of different—and speedier—methods. I have a very handy pan that is heavy and ridged and requires little if any fat. I also use my broiler to grill. I heat it to hot, place the food on a pan (preferably foil-lined), and place the pan several inches under the broiler. I also have a flat nonstick pan that will fit over two burners that I use as a grill or griddle. I've also used a tiny hibachi as a grill; it doesn't use much charcoal and can be ready to cook in just 15 minutes or so.

FIVE-SPICE PORK LOIN

PORK LOINS
Have the butcher halve a loin of pork and prepare one side as chops and the other half as a loin roast. Marinate the loin for later in the week (see Five Spice Pork Loin) and fix a fast- broiled or pan-fried chop recipe the first night's supper. This sort of planning is good for the budget and the psyche.

Now that the Asian flavors are so much a part of American cuisine, I like making rubs and marinades for non-Asian dishes like this roast. It cries out for dinner guests.

The boneless center portion of the pork loin is very often available in my grocery store. It's a very handy piece of meat as it cooks unattended and reheats well. This will taste great even if you don't have time to let it marinate overnight. The use of prepared sauces gives great flavor for little effort.

SEASONING RUB
½ tablespoon Szechuan sauce
1 tablespoon hoisin sauce
2 teaspoons five-spice powder
¼ cup chopped fresh parsley

1 teaspoon hot mustard
Salt
Freshly ground black pepper

1 2-pound boneless pork loin

To make the rub, combine the Szechuan sauce, hoisin sauce, five-spice powder, parsley, hot mustard, and salt and pepper to taste in a food processor. Purée until the parsley is chopped fine. Rub the pork loin until well covered. Marinate the meat at least 1 hour to overnight, if possible, covered or in a large resealable plastic bag, in the refrigerator.

Preheat the oven to 350°F. Grease a shallow baking pan.

Place the roast in the prepared pan and roast to an internal temperature of 145°F. to 150°F. on a meat thermometer, about 35 to 40 minutes. It will take less time if the roast was at room temperature when placed in the oven. Let the roast rest for 10 minutes before carving.

Serves 6 to 8

NOTE: *To speed up cooking time, place the roast in the oven while preheating. This will bring it back to room temperature.*

CRANBERRY TENDERLOIN OF PORK

Aroma plays a major part in this lovely entrée, which is redolent of fall. It smells so good, in fact, everyone will think you've been home cooking all day, rather than just rushing in and cooking in a hurry.

The marinating is best done ahead, but if there is no time, just add the marinade mixture when called for. If the meat is frozen, you could easily slice it into medallions while it is still partially frozen, then add to the bag with the marinade.

2 ½- to 1-pound pork tenderloins
Salt
Freshly ground black pepper
1 cup cranberry juice

¼ teaspoon ground cinnamon
¼ teaspoon ground cloves
2 tablespoons vegetable oil
¼ cup heavy cream

Slice the tenderloins into 1-inch medallions. Place between 2 pieces of plastic wrap on a board and flatten with a heavy mallet, frying pan, or skillet. Season with salt and pepper. Place the tenderloins in a resealable plastic bag. Add the cranberry juice, cinnamon, and cloves. Marinate at least 1 hour or overnight, if possible. Remove the tenderloins from the marinade and shake off.

Heat the oil in a large skillet on high. Add the tenderloin slices and sauté quickly, 2 to 3 minutes each side. Do not overcrowd the pan. Remove the meat when done and set aside. Add the marinade and bring to the boil. Reduce by half, about 5 minutes. Add the cream, bring to the boil, and reduce the sauce by half, about 5 minutes. Return the meat to the sauce to coat and heat through. Serve hot.

Serves 4 to 6

Pork and Onions with Pepper Jelly Sauce

Margaret Ann, my former assistant and recipe tester, created this dish with me one day. We both always loved the pork with pepper jelly recipe in *New Southern Cooking* and wanted to see if we couldn't make it even better. With the cream it is quite elegant, but you could certainly omit the cream for a fast, zippy family meal. Try to have your onions sliced ahead of time or slice them while the meat is browning.

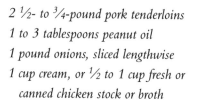

2 ½- to ¾-pound pork tenderloins
1 to 3 tablespoons peanut oil
1 pound onions, sliced lengthwise
1 cup cream, or ½ to 1 cup fresh or
  canned chicken stock or broth

½ cup hot pepper jelly
Salt
Freshly ground black pepper

Slice the meat crosswise into ½- to ¾-inch-thick slices. Heat the oil in a large skillet. Over medium heat brown the pork slices on one side, turn, and brown on the other, about 5 minutes in all. Remove the meat from the pan, add the onions, and cook until soft and browned, about 15 minutes. Stir in the cream, then add the jelly, and stir until melted. Bring to the boil and boil until somewhat reduced, about 2 minutes. Season with salt and pepper to taste. Return the pork to the pan and heat through with the sauce. Serve immediately.

Serves 4 to 6

TOMATO CAPER PORK TENDERLOIN

I further decreased the cooking time of this very savory, flavorful dish, which is adapted from one in Carol Cutler's *Cuisine Rapide*, by substituting boneless tenderloin cutlets for pork chops and flattening the medallions. Pork cutlets are available prepackaged in some markets.

2 1- to 2-pound pork tenderloins, cut
  into 1-inch thick rounds
2 tablespoons butter
Salt
Freshly ground black pepper
¼ cup sherry or fresh or canned chicken
  stock or broth

2 tablespoons chopped fresh parsley
1½ tablespoons capers, chopped
4 anchovy fillets, chopped (optional)
1 cup crushed tomatoes
2 tablespoons tomato paste
1 tablespoon finely chopped fresh basil

Flatten the pork medallions between 2 pieces of plastic wrap with a heavy frying pan or the side of a large knife or cleaver.

Heat the butter in a large skillet over medium-high heat. Season the cutlets with salt and pepper on both sides. Add the meat to the pan and brown on one side, 2 to 3 minutes, then turn and brown the second side. Remove the meat from the pan and keep warm. Add the sherry or stock and stir to scrape up and dissolve the pork bits from the bottom of the pan. Add the parsley, capers, anchovy fillets if using, tomatoes, and tomato paste. Stir well to combine. Reduce the heat to simmer and cook 3 to 5 minutes. Return the meat to the pan and heat through, 3 to 5 minutes. Add the basil and season to taste with salt and pepper.

Serves 6

Pasta with Sausage and Bitter Greens ■ *Pasta with Shellfish and Sugar Snaps* ■ *Quick Clam Spaghetti* ■ *Spaghetti with Mussels* ■ *Spaghetti Frittata* ■ *Elizabeth Vaeth's Pasta with Peppers* ■ *Risotto with Shrimp* ■ *Fettuccine with Salmon Cream* ■ *Fast and Easy Rosemary*

PASTA, PIZZA, AND OTHER LIGHT REPASTS

Fettuccine ■ *Lemon-Basil Pasta* ■ *Linguine with Four Cheeses* ■ *Parsley and Butter Tortellini* ■ *Roasted Tomato Sauce with Linguine* ■ *Omelets* ■ *Bacon and Onion Pizza* ■ *Mexican Goat Cheese Pizza* ■ *Black Bean Burgers* ■ *Hot or Cold Grilled Chicken Salad*

SUNDAY DINNER just wouldn't seem the same without a pot roast or roasted chicken, but for busy weeknights I'm often happy with a less substantial meal. A plate of pasta, a golden omelet filled with a few savory tidbits, or a quickly assembled and baked pizza fill me up without slowing me down and need only a salad to round out the plate. Best of all, many of these light repasts are wonderful ways to use up odds and ends or leftovers, reducing the time I spend in the market as well as at the stove.

Pasta in all its marvelously varied forms has been the salvation of many last-minute cooks. I have an instant hot water heater in my sink, and it is close to being my favorite kitchen gadget. If you are reluctant to make that investment, bringing two half pans of water to the boil (one can be a tea kettle) will be faster than heating one large pot of water. Once the pasta's going, you can make a fast sauce with butter, oil, cheese, tomatoes, even a vinaigrette in the time it takes to cook the pasta.

I also make twice as much pasta as I need and save half for another time. (I don't feel apologetic to my Italian friends; I just don't invite them for the leftover kind.) Cooked pasta can be reheated in the microwave, with a quick dip into boiling water in a metal colander, or by tossing in butter or oil in a large pan over high heat. And, of course, it makes a welcome salad. Cooked vegetables and meats can be cut into strips or pieces and added to the pasta and served hot or cold with an appropriate hot or cold sauce.

The stuffed pastas, like raviolis and tortellinis, are ideal for your "no-brainer" list. Sold packaged for pantry, refrigerator, or freezer in exotic new flavors, they lend themselves to both hot and cold presentations and can be changed instantly simply by varying the sauce.

With practice you can cook your vegetables in the boiling water, adding them according to the length of their cooking time, then add angel hair pasta or other thin or small pasta, for just a few minutes, then drain the whole shebang at once; just add a bit of oil and herbs and you are done, with only one pan to clean.

Pasta with Sausage and Bitter Greens

Most any green vegetable will go with this dish. It's my standby recipe for using what's in the house, in a hurry.

1 pound penne or other pasta

1 tablespoon olive oil or butter

1 pound Italian pork or turkey sausage

1 cup chopped broccoli rabe, chard, arugula, spinach, broccoli florets, or zucchini

1 cup sliced mushrooms

1 carrot, grated

1 tablespoon finely chopped fresh basil

1 tablespoon finely chopped fresh oregano

1 28-ounce can crushed tomatoes, with juices (optional)

½ cup grated imported Parmesan cheese

Salt

Freshly ground black pepper

Bring a large pot of water to a rolling boil. Add the pasta and stir. Return to the boil and cook, uncovered, until al dente, according to package directions. Drain well.

In a Dutch oven heat the olive oil over medium heat (omit if using pork sausage). Add the meat and brown lightly. Remove the meat and set aside. Add the green vegetable, mushrooms, carrot, basil, and oregano, and cook in the pan drippings over medium heat until softened, about 3 to 5 minutes. Add the crushed tomatoes and their juices if using and stir well to combine. Return the meat and drained pasta to the pot and add the Parmesan. Simmer uncovered 5 to 10 minutes. Season to taste with salt and pepper. Serve hot.

Serves 4

SAVING SAUSAGE

Once found only at Italian delis, Italian sausage can now be found in almost any grocery store. I buy extra whenever it's on sale and freeze it; four links fit nicely into a sandwich-size resealable bag. Keep them around to throw on the grill with some sliced vegetables for an impromptu Italian-style picnic or to add flavor to lentil soup. You need not defrost them first if they are to be pansautéed in your recipe; just be sure to puncture them to allow fat and steam to escape.

PASTA WITH SHELLFISH AND SUGAR SNAPS

This dish is a meal in itself. Serve with a crusty Italian bread or focaccia and fresh fruit and cheese for dessert. It also makes a very attractive first course for 8. Do not freeze.

1 pound spaghetti or angel hair pasta
¼ cup olive oil
1 pound bay scallops
1 pound shrimp, shelled and deveined
Salt
Freshly ground black pepper
4 garlic cloves, peeled and chopped

2 teaspoons red pepper flakes
4 cups sugar snap peas or snow peas (see Note)
3 fresh or canned tomatoes, finely chopped
½ cup grated imported Parmesan cheese (optional)

Bring a large pot of water to a rolling boil. Add the pasta and stir. Return to the boil and cook, uncovered, until al dente, according to package directions. Drain well.

While the pasta is cooking, heat the olive oil in a large Dutch oven. Add the scallops and shrimp and sauté until the scallops turn opaque and the shrimp turn pink and are just beginning to curl, about 2 to 3 minutes. Remove from the pan with a slotted spoon and season to taste with salt and pepper. Add the garlic and red pepper flakes to the pan and cook for 2 minutes. Add the sugar snaps and sauté for 2 minutes. Remove from the heat, cover the pan, and let sit for 5 minutes.

In a large serving bowl, combine the tomatoes with the scallops and shrimp. Add the hot pasta and the sugar snaps. Toss and serve sprinkled with the Parmesan cheese, if using.

Serves 4

NOTE: *Four cups of cleaned spinach, stems removed, can be substituted for the sugar snaps; add to the sautéed garlic, remove from the heat immediately, and let sit for 5 minutes. Proceed as above.*

QUICK CLAM SPAGHETTI

My friend Margaret Ann Surber, who has worked with me off and on for nearly fifteen years, prepares this meal for her family when they arrive late and hungry at their mountain cabin. She can make it quickly from the pantry, adding fresh parsley and thyme from her garden. She uses angel hair pasta because it is the quickest to cook. Some say no Italian would mix Parmesan with clams—but it certainly enhances the meal if you "don't know any better" and are hungry and tired!

1 pound angel hair pasta
1 to 2 tablespoons olive oil
1 small onion, finely chopped
2 to 4 garlic cloves, peeled and finely
   chopped
3 to 4 6½-ounce cans clams, drained,
   juice reserved

¼ cup dry white wine or vermouth
   (optional)
2 tablespoons chopped fresh thyme
¼ cup chopped fresh parsley
Salt
Red pepper flakes
½ cup grated imported Parmesan cheese
   (optional)

Bring a large pot of water to a rolling boil. Add the pasta and stir. Return to the boil and cook, uncovered, until al dente, according to package directions. Drain well.

While the pasta is cooking, in a large skillet, heat the oil over medium heat. Add the onion and garlic, and cook until soft, about 7 to 10 minutes. Add the reserved clam juice and wine, if using, and boil until reduced by half, about 8 minutes. Remove from the heat and stir in the clams, thyme, and parsley. Taste and, if necessary, add salt. Be careful—sometimes the clam juice is salty enough on its own. Add red pepper flakes to taste, toss well with the pasta, and serve hot. Pass the Parmesan cheese if desired.

Serves 4

SPAGHETTI WITH MUSSELS

MUSSELS
Farm-raised mussels need only a last-minute check: I use a sharp knife to remove the beard, and then I give them a last rinse in cold water before scooping them up with a strainer to add to the saucepan. They steam open over the liquid of your choice—white wine and herbs, tomato juice, chicken or clam broth, beer, even water—in less than 10 minutes. Serve simply in the shell with bread to sop up the cooking liquid.

Remove leftovers from their shells, and toss with a mustardy vinaigrette for a sophisticated seafood salad.

This is about as easy a meal as you can make, with a great deal of cachet! My local grocery store carries 2-pound bags of farm-raised mussels, which can be debearded in a matter of minutes. Both flavorful and beautiful, this spaghetti will stay at the top of your "what's for dinner list." It can be reheated in the microwave in 5 minutes.

1 pound spaghetti or other long pasta
¼ cup olive oil
4 garlic cloves, peeled and chopped
1 28-ounce can plum tomatoes, drained and coarsely chopped, or 4 cups cherry or Roma tomatoes, halved
2 tablespoons chopped fresh basil
2 tablespoons chopped fresh parsley
1 hot red pepper, seeded and chopped

Salt
Freshly ground black pepper
48 to 60 (about 2 pounds) live mussels, scrubbed and debearded

GARNISH
1 tablespoon chopped fresh parsley or basil

Bring a large pot of water to a rolling boil. Add the pasta and stir. Return to the boil and cook, uncovered, until al dente, according to package directions. Drain well.

In a 5-quart saucepan, heat the olive oil over medium-high heat. Add the garlic, tomatoes, basil, parsley, hot pepper, and salt and pepper to taste. Sauté 5 minutes, stirring to prevent sticking. Add the cleaned mussels, cover the pot, and cook until the mussels have opened, about 5 to 7 minutes. Discard any mussels that do not open. Pour the sauce and mussels over the pasta, toss well, and sprinkle with the chopped parsley or basil.

Serves 6

SPAGHETTI FRITTATA

A frittata is essentially an Italian omelet, with a beautiful browned exterior and moist middle. It can be made with eggs alone, but adding cheese, onion, and herbs makes it a little more exciting and substantial, and it's a smart way to use up leftovers. The first time I made this, it featured some leftover spaghetti and everyone enjoyed it.

½ pound spaghetti

6 eggs

1 cup grated sharp cheddar or moz-
  zarella cheese

¾ cup grated imported Parmesan cheese

2 teaspoons salt

Freshly ground black pepper

4 to 6 tablespoons butter

1 garlic clove, peeled and finely chopped

Preheat the oven to 350°F.

Bring a large pot of water to a rolling boil. Add the pasta and stir. Return to the boil and cook, uncovered, until al dente, according to package directions. Drain well.

Beat together the eggs and cheeses. Season to taste with salt and pepper. Heat the butter over medium heat in a frying pan with an ovenproof handle. Add the garlic and sauté briefly, then add the spaghetti and combine. Pour the egg mixture over the spaghetti and mix well with a fork. Cook about 2 minutes, then transfer to the oven and bake without flipping until the eggs are set, 10 to 15 minutes.

Serves 4 to 6

EGG SUBSTITUTES

If you're short on eggs, a hint I came across in *The Regional Italian Kitchen* by Nika Hazelton can help out in a pinch. It says "For each missing egg, and not for more than 2 eggs, blend together 2 teaspoons flour with 3 tablespoons water or milk. The result is not perfect, but it will do in an emergency."

You can also make a smaller frittata, prepared like a pancake in a skillet or griddle. The frittata should be ¾ to 1 inch thick to ensure the desired texture.

ELIZABETH VAETH'S PASTA WITH PEPPERS

The great color of this dish makes it especially appealing to kids, as do the unusual pasta shapes. The short preparation time makes it easy on harried working mothers. To vary it I sauté strips of boneless chicken breasts in the oil and add some marjoram.

1 12-ounce package tube-shaped or multicolored pasta
¼ to ½ cup olive oil
½ red bell pepper, seeded and sliced into strips or chopped

½ yellow bell pepper, seeded and sliced into strips or chopped
2 garlic cloves, peeled and chopped
1 cup fresh broccoli florets
1 cup grated imported Parmesan cheese

Bring a large pot of water to a rolling boil. Add the pasta and stir. Return to the boil and cook, uncovered, until al dente, according to package directions. Drain well.

While the pasta is cooking, heat the olive oil in a medium skillet over medium heat. Add the peppers and garlic and sauté until tender but not browned, about 5 minutes; set aside. Cook the broccoli in boiling water or in the boiling pasta water with the pasta for 5 minutes.

Drain the pasta and broccoli and transfer to a serving bowl. Mix in the peppers and garlic. Sprinkle generously with the Parmesan and serve hot.

Serves 4

NOTE: *This can be made with cooked, leftover pasta. Microwave the broccoli for 3 minutes, then add it and the pasta to the skillet with the peppers. Toss over medium heat until heated through.*

RISOTTO WITH SHRIMP

Although they require a fair amount of "people time" I still consider satisfying risottos good spur-of-the-moment fare. If you add vegetables and a bit of meat or fish, a risotto needs only a salad or green vegetable to make a special family supper. As a side dish for a company meal, it will serve 6 to 8. Shrimp stock gives this rendition its wonderfully rich flavor. Do seek out a source for Arborio rice; you can use a medium- or long-grain rice, but you will not get the silky, creamy texture the Italian short-grained rice is famous for. You can substitute salmon for the shrimp with equally good results. This reheats in the microwave.

SHRIMP STOCK
I keep the water in which I've boiled shrimp and use it for stock. Alternatively, in a stockpot, combine 36 crushed shrimp shells, 2 quarts water, 1 small onion cut in half, 1 small carrot cut in quarters, 3 parsley stalks, 2 lemon wedges, and salt and pepper to taste. Bring to the boil, reduce to a simmer, and cook until the liquid is reduced to 6 cups. Shrimp shells can be frozen up to 2 months; keep a resealable plastic bag in your freezer and add to it whenever you peel shrimp.

3 tablespoons butter

3 garlic cloves, peeled and chopped

2 onions, chopped

4 green onions, chopped

2 tablespoons fresh lemon juice

2 cups Arborio rice

6 cups shrimp stock (see sidebar), at a
   simmer

36 medium to large shrimp, peeled and
   deveined, shells reserved for stock

2 teaspoons finely chopped fresh thyme

Salt

Freshly ground black pepper

2 tablespoons chopped fresh parsley

¾ cup grated imported Parmesan cheese
   (optional)

Melt the butter in a large Dutch oven. Add the garlic, onions, and green onions and sauté over medium heat for 2 minutes. Add the lemon juice and the rice and cook for 2 to 3 minutes until the rice is coated with the butter and begins to look opaque. Add the hot shrimp stock ½ cup at a time, stirring constantly, until the liquid has been absorbed by the rice. It should take about 20 to 25 minutes to cook the rice to a creamy consistency. When you add the final ½ cup of stock, add the raw shrimp, thyme, and salt and pepper to taste. The shrimp will cook in about 3 minutes. Before serving, fluff with a fork and sprinkle with the parsley and optional Parmesan, if desired.

Serves 4 to 6

FETTUCCINE WITH SALMON CREAM

REHEATING PASTA

The very idea is anathema to some, but you really *can* cook pasta ahead and reheat it just before serving—if you follow certain rules. Most important, undercook the pasta slightly; it should be al dente, with a clearly visible white core at the center of each pasta strand. Don't allow the pasta to stand in its cooking water, where it will continue to cook; drain well and toss with a small amount of oil to keep the strands separate. At serving time, place the pasta in a colander and immerse in boiling water for 30 seconds or add directly to your hot sauce or butter or oil and toss over a high flame for 30 seconds.

This is one of the best reasons I know for keeping a good Parmesan in the freezer and cream in the fridge. I love it with salmon, but it makes a lovely vegetarian entrée with broccoli, peas, or asparagus added to the pasta water—or substitute cooked chicken or crabmeat if you like. Spinach or multicolored fettuccine makes for a more interesting plate, but any pasta will do if you are "in a tight" for time.

1 pound fettuccine

3 tablespoons butter

1 cup heavy cream

8 ounces smoked salmon, cut in strips

1 teaspoon chopped fresh dill

Freshly grated nutmeg

Salt

Freshly ground black pepper

1/2 cup grated imported Parmesan cheese

Bring a large pot of water to a rolling boil. Add the pasta and stir. Return to the boil and cook, uncovered, until al dente, according to package directions. Drain well.

While the pasta cooks, combine the butter and cream in a large skillet and bring to the boil over medium-high heat. Lower the heat and simmer until the cream has reduced by half, about 5 minutes. Stir in the salmon and dill, and season to taste with nutmeg, salt, and pepper. Add the drained pasta and Parmesan and toss until the pasta is well coated. Season with salt and pepper to taste and serve immediately.

Serves 6

FAST AND EASY ROSEMARY FETTUCCINE

I love a recipe that leaves only one pot to clean and can be on the table in 15 minutes—who wouldn't? This dish reheats well in the microwave.

1 pound fettuccine

¼ cup rosemary compound butter (see sidebar)

2 tablespoons chopped fresh basil

2 tablespoons grated Parmesan cheese

1 tablespoon balsamic vinegar

Salt

Freshly ground black pepper

Bring a large pot of water to a rolling boil. Add the pasta and stir. Return to the boil and cook, uncovered, until al dente, according to package directions. Drain well and return to the same pot. Add the butter, basil, Parmesan, and balsamic vinegar and toss thoroughly. Season to taste with salt and pepper.

Serves 6

COMPOUND BUTTER

Compound butter is a mixture of butter and two or more ingredients, such as lemon juice, garlic, and/or herbs. The food processor makes it a snap. For rosemary compound butter, pulse 3 tablespoons rosemary in the food processor until bruised. Add ½ cup (1 stick) butter at room temperature and 1 peeled garlic clove. Purée until smooth. Form the mixture into a cylinder and refrigerate or freeze until needed.

LEMON-BASIL PASTA

G remolata, that heady combination of parsley, lemon peel, and garlic that accents many Italian recipes like osso buco, is the basis of this dish. I like to keep some in the freezer for a quick addition to recipes. The zesty flavor of this pasta makes it appealing as a side dish for grilled meats or vegetables, or add vegetables for a vegetarian main course.

½ pound pasta, any variety

Grated or chopped peel (no white attached) of 1 lemon

2 to 3 garlic cloves, peeled and finely chopped

½ cup finely chopped fresh parsley

2 tablespoons extra-virgin olive oil

2 tablespoons finely chopped fresh basil

Salt

Freshly ground black pepper

QUICKER ZESTING

Although there are special tools designed just for removing citrus rind, I find a good vegetable peeler does the job just as well, especially if you need a substantial quantity of zest. Remove long strips of zest, being careful not to take any of the bitter white pith, then chop finely with a sharp knife or whirl in a mini food processor. (It chops better in the processor if left on the counter to air-dry briefly.) Store leftovers in the refrigerator for up to 3 days in a small resealable plastic bag with all the air pressed out.

Bring a large pot of water to a rolling boil. Add the pasta and stir. Return to the boil and cook, uncovered, until al dente, according to package directions. Drain well and transfer to a heated serving bowl.

While the pasta is cooking, make the gremolata by tossing together the lemon peel, garlic, and parsley in a small bowl. Add the olive oil to the pasta while it is still hot and toss well. Add the gremolata and basil and toss to combine. Season to taste with salt and pepper. Serve warm or at room temperature.

Serves 4

LINGUINE WITH FOUR CHEESES

This decadent dish is super easy, rich, and smooth, but it does not reheat well once the cheese is added. The cheeses specified below are merely suggestions. Let your preferences and the contents of your refrigerator dictate.

1 pound linguine
¼ pound Swiss chees e
¼ pound sharp cheddar
¼ pound mozzarella
1 garlic clove, peeled and finely chopped
1 cup milk

¼ cup (½ stick) butter, cut into small
 pieces
1 cup grated imported Parmesan cheese
Salt
Freshly ground black pepper

Bring a large pot of water to a rolling boil. Add the pasta and stir. Return to the boil and cook, uncovered, until al dente, according to package directions. Drain well.

While the pasta is cooking, cut the Swiss, cheddar, and mozzarella into small pieces. Combine with the garlic and milk in a large microwave-safe bowl and microwave on high 2 to 3 minutes or cook over low heat in a saucepan 5 minutes. The cheeses should be soft, but not melted.

Add the drained linguine to the cheese-milk mixture and toss together. Add the butter and Parmesan and toss again. Season to taste with salt and pepper.

Serves 4 to 6

Parsley and Butter Tortellini

This recipe requires little if any real thought but is a wonderful side dish and always seems special. It is super quick and reheats well. Vary the herb to create something different—basil, oregano, or rosemary would work equally well. Leftover bits of meat, salmon, or vegetables will make it more substantial. Double for a main course.

3 quarts water

1 9-ounce package stuffed tortellini or ravioli

3 tablespoons finely chopped fresh parsley or other herb

1 garlic clove, peeled and finely chopped

1 tablespoon butter

Salt

Freshly ground black pepper

Bring a large pot of water to a rolling boil. Add the pasta and stir. Return to the boil and cook, uncovered, until al dente, according to package directions. Drain well and return to the pot. Add the parsley, garlic, and butter and toss gently. Season to taste with salt and pepper. Serve hot.

Serves 4

STUFFED PASTAS
Prepared stuffed pastas, whether fresh, frozen, or boxed, are wonderful to keep on hand. Try different fillings, like pumpkin, Parmesan and herb, lobster and cheese, or porcini mushrooms. They can be boiled, then quickly sautéed in oil, topped with a cream and Gorgonzola sauce, or floated in a broth. They don't need a recipe but certainly can make a meal.

ROASTED TOMATO SAUCE WITH LINGUINE

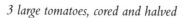

Bits of smoked, charred tomato give this light-bodied sauce its intense flavor. The vegetables are roasted and then puréed, giving the sauce a pleasing texture and fresh taste that is quite different from a long-simmered tomato sauce. Start the vegetables first; by the time the pasta water boils and the pasta cooks the vegetables will be ready for the food processor. This dish freezes well and can easily be multiplied up.

3 large tomatoes, cored and halved
2 large onions, sliced ½ inch thick
½ pound linguine
3 to 4 fresh red peppers, roasted or
   1 14½-ounce jar roasted red peppers

1 tablespoon chopped fresh rosemary
1 clove garlic, peeled and finely chopped
Salt
Freshly ground black pepper

Preheat the oven to 450°F.

Place the tomatoes and onions in a roasting pan. Roast for 20 to 25 minutes, then turn the oven to broil and broil the vegetables for 10 minutes to char the tops. Meanwhile, bring a large pot of water to a rolling boil. Add the pasta and stir. Return to the boil and cook, uncovered, until al dente, according to package directions. Drain well.

Transfer the roasted vegetables to the bowl of a food processor and purée. Add the red peppers, rosemary, and garlic and purée. Season to taste with salt and pepper. Toss with the linguine and serve hot.

Serves 4

PASTA NO-BRAINERS
Five-minute pasta toppers: To an 8-ounce jar of your favorite prepared marinara sauce add
• a can of drained tuna and chopped black olives
• an 8-ounce bag of frozen shrimp and chopped fresh basil
• chunks of sautéed or grilled zucchini, yellow squash, and onion
• ½ cup heavy cream and 1 cup frozen tiny peas
• ½ cup ricotta cheese, 6 strips crisp bacon, crumbled, 8 ounces of cleaned fresh spinach, cut in thin strips
Heat through, combine with hot pasta, and serve!

OMELETS

Omelets are a nice change from meaty main courses, and they adapt easily to many different fillings—every desperate cook should know how to make one! They make a nice lunch or a light supper, served with a salad. Have your filling ready before you get started, as the omelet is done in minutes; here I offer a choice of Mexican or Mushroom and Herb fillings. A special omelet pan isn't necessary, but a nonstick skillet does make life (and cleanup) easier.

BASIC OMELET	⅛ teaspoon salt
3 eggs	*1 tablespoon butter*
1 tablespoon water	

Whisk together the eggs, water, and salt. Heat the butter in a skillet until it just starts to turn color. Add the egg mixture. Move the skillet around, forward and backward, to allow the uncooked egg mixture to cover the skillet bottom. When the eggs start to solidify, place the cooked filling mixture of your choice on one side of the eggs. Fold the omelet over the filling and slide onto a platter. Serve immediately.

Serves 2

MEXICAN FILLING	*Salt*
1 tablespoon butter	*Freshly ground black pepper*
⅛ teaspoon ground cumin	
2 green onions, chopped	
½ red bell pepper, seeded and chopped	*TOPPING*
1 tomato, peeled, seeded, and chopped	*1 cup salsa*
1 teaspoon chopped fresh oregano	*½ cup grated Monterey Jack cheese*

Melt the butter in a large skillet. Add the cumin and heat until fragrant. Add the green onions, red bell pepper, tomato, and oregano. Season to taste with salt and pepper and sauté quickly until just done, 2 to 3 minutes.

Top the filled omelet with the salsa and cheese.

NO-BRAINER OMELET STUFFERS

If beating some eggs is all the cooking you're up to, keep these no-cook fillings in mind: Leftover Chinese take-out (I love Mu Shu Pork); canned chili and chopped green onions; cottage or yogurt cheese mixed with fresh or dried herbs; slivers of smoked salmon and cream cheese; sautéed onions and ham with grated Gruyère or Emmentaler; bits of leftover grilled vegetables with a touch of goat cheese; and every kid's favorite, grape jelly.

MUSHROOM AND HERB FILLING
1 tablespoon butter
1 medium onion, chopped
1 cup small button mushrooms, sliced

½ tablespoon finely chopped fresh parsley
½ tablespoon finely chopped fresh basil or tarragon
Salt
Freshly ground black pepper

Melt the butter in a large skillet. Add the onion, mushrooms, parsley, and basil. Sauté quickly until just done, 2 to 3 minutes. Season to taste with salt and pepper.

BACON AND ONION PIZZA

PRESTO! PIZZAS!
Pizza is a great last-minute starter or meal that can be thrown together with whatever's on hand. Bits of this and that—leftover chicken, veggies, herbs and spices, even potatoes—with a slather of sauce and a sprinkling of cheese can suddenly become a unique treat. Prebaked crusts cut prep time down to nothing, but you can also buy unbaked, frozen crusts, or fresh pizza dough to roll out and shape yourself, both of which will require a bit more time in the oven.

Premade, prebaked pizza crusts are such lifesavers. With a premade crust, it is even faster to make your own pizza, topped with healthful, enticing add-ons, than to order out and wait for delivery! This combination of flavors makes for a delicious, nearly instant pizza.

6 slices bacon, cut into 1-inch pieces
3 medium onions, sliced
3 tablespoons finely chopped fresh parsley
1 14½-ounce can salsa-style tomatoes, drained

Salt
Freshly ground black pepper
1 10-inch prebaked pizza crust
1 tablespoon olive oil

Preheat the oven to 450°F.

In a large skillet, cook the bacon over medium heat until soft. Add the onions to the bacon and cook until they are soft and brown, about 6 or 7 minutes. Add the parsley and tomatoes and combine. Season to taste with salt and pepper.

Place the pizza crust on a large baking sheet. Brush with oil, and spoon the filling on top, spreading almost but not all the way to the edges. Bake until hot and bubbling, 8 to 10 minutes.

Serves 4 to 6

Mexican Goat Cheese Pizza

It is perhaps a misnomer to call these sophisticated little rounds "pizzas," but whether you call them pizzas, quesadillas, or open-faced sandwiches, don't wait for a Mexican dinner party to make them; they are nice for a Sunday night supper or an unusual hors d'oeuvre. Chorizo is a spicy, red, dried Spanish sausage. Pepperoni or other spicy dried meat may be substituted.

1 to 3 tablespoons vegetable oil
8 to 10 corn or flour tortillas (4 to 6
*   if using large flour tortillas)*
8 ounces Montrachet or other soft goat
*   cheese*
½ pound hot chorizo sausage or pepper-
*   oni, roughly chopped or hot bulk fresh*
*   sausage, crumbled and cooked*

1 to 3 tablespoons chopped fresh cilantro
*   (optional)*
Small hot peppers, such as jalapeños,
*   fresh or pickled, seeded and chopped*
1 tomato, peeled, seeded, and chopped
*   (optional)*

TORTILLAS
Think of tortillas as handy, all-purpose wrappers that can transform leftover meat, vegetables, and cheese scraps into a last-minute enchilada, taco, or pizza in minutes. I keep tortillas in the freezer at all times; they defrost in seconds and are enormously versatile. Tortillas are also available in cans, which have an equally long shelf life and are ready to use as is.

Preheat the broiler. Brush a baking sheet with oil or spray with nonstick cooking spray.

Heat 1 tablespoon of the oil in a nonstick skillet. Add the tortillas one at a time and fry on one side until speckled with brown, 1 minute or less. Turn and fry the second side. Repeat, adding oil as needed until all the tortillas are toasted, stacking them on a plate. (The tortillas can also be crisped in the oven but will not be quite as tasty.)

Break the cheese into chunks and sprinkle it over the tortillas. Cover the cheese with some of the chorizo or pepperoni, cilantro if using, jalapeño peppers, and the tomato if using. Place the tortillas on the prepared baking sheet and broil until bubbly, about 3 minutes. Serve whole for entrée portions, or halve or quarter to make appetizer portions.

Serves 4 to 6

BLACK BEAN BURGERS

The spices and seasonings in this protein-packed, meatless burger will wow the most jaded carnivore. The number of ingredients is in inverse ratio to the difficulty of the dish—the more ingredients in this case, the easier. The beans tend to hold their shape better if you use dry beans that have been soaked overnight and cooked gently about 2 hours. (This may be done in advance. Put the beans on to cook one night while you prepare the evening meal, then drain the beans, refrigerate, and use for a couple of meals.) If you use canned beans, drain them very well as the patties will not hold their shape if there is too much liquid. These burgers do not reheat well.

*4 cups cooked black beans, well drained,
  fresh or canned*
1 red onion, finely chopped
*1 red bell pepper, seeded and finely
  chopped*
*1 poblano pepper, roasted, peeled,
  seeded, and chopped (optional)*
1 tablespoon ground cumin
1 tablespoon chili powder
2 tablespoons chopped fresh cilantro
¼ to ½ teaspoon cayenne pepper

Salt
Freshly ground black pepper
1 tablespoon peanut oil
Whole wheat buns or pita bread

G A R N I S H
Lettuce leaves
Tomato slices
*Tomatillo Salsa (page 29) or prepared
  salsa*

In a large bowl, mash the beans with a potato masher or the back of a spoon. Mix in the red onion, red bell pepper, poblano pepper, cumin, chili powder, cilantro, cayenne, and salt and pepper to taste.

Heat the oil in a heavy skillet over medium-high heat. Form the mixture into 8 thick patties and fry, about 2 minutes per side. Serve hot on whole wheat buns or pita bread with lettuce, tomato, and the salsa of your choice.

Serves 6 to 8

Variation: These delicious burgers can also be served open-faced on a toasted bun bottom and sprinkled with feta or a crumbly Mexican cheese with salsa on the side.

HOT OR COLD GRILLED CHICKEN SALAD

Salad combined with grilled meat or poultry is a contemporary take on the all-in-one meal—casual yet memorable, and can be served hot or cold. Many times when I heat up the grill for dinner I cook more chicken or meat than I need so I can refrigerate or even freeze the extra, then pull it out when I need something for a quick meal. In addition to greens, I've successfully combined leftover pasta, rice, and couscous with the chicken.

SALAD TIME-SAVER
Prewashed and packaged greens, including spinach and mesclun salad mixtures, are now available in many produce departments. These are real time-savers and also eliminate waste if you like to mix several greens in your salads but won't be able to use an entire head of each.

4 boneless, skinless chicken breasts, grilled (see basic recipe, page 74)

½ red onion, sliced

½ cup pecans or walnuts, chopped

2 tablespoons finely chopped fresh thyme

3 to 4 tablespoons finely chopped fresh parsley

2 tablespoons finely chopped fresh cilantro

1 cup Basic Vinaigrette (page 43)

1 tablespoon soy sauce

1 tablespoon sesame oil

1 tablespoon lime juice

4 cups mixed lettuce (red leaf, butter, bibb)

Let the grilled chicken breasts return to room temperature if they have been refrigerated. Slice crosswise into ⅛-inch-thick slices and place in a medium mixing bowl. Add the red onion, pecans or walnuts, thyme, parsley, and cilantro. Pour the vinaigrette over the chicken mixture. Add the soy sauce, sesame oil, and lime juice, and toss well. May be made up to a day ahead to this point.

Arrange the lettuce on individual plates or a platter. Top with the chicken mixture.

Serves 4 to 6

Asparagus in Vinaigrette ■ *Broccoli Stir-Fry* ■ *Zesty Grated Carrots* ■
Celery and Walnuts ■ *Minted Hot Cucumbers* ■ *Peas and Tomatoes* ■
Flash-Fried Spinach ■ *Quick Squash Sauté* ■ *Baked Rosemary Squash*
■ *Grilled Zucchini* ■ *Layered Zucchini and Tomatoes* ■ *Zucchini and Celery*
Sauté ■ *Julienned Gingered Vegetables* ■ *Tricolor Stir-Fried Vegetables*

VEGETABLES
AND
SIDE DISHES

■ *Green Beans with Orange Vinaigrette* ■ *Basil and Cheese Stuffed*
Tomatoes ■ *Sautéed Mushrooms and Vegetables* ■ *Spinach Sauce* ■
Garlic Roasted Potatoes ■ *Herbed Mashed Potatoes* ■ *Potato*
Pancakes ■ *Scalloped Sweet Potatoes* ■ *Ribboned Potatoes* ■ *Bulgur*
Pilaf ■ *Spiced Couscous* ■ *Fried Rice* ■ *Baked Mushroom Rice*

SIDE DISHES can sometimes get lost in the shuffle when it comes to planning quick meals, and indeed there are many times when a loaf of bread, some prewashed salad mix, or a can of baked beans is all the side dish you need. But with just a little more effort, it is a simple matter to make vegetable dishes or grains that make a meal a bit more special. When I was growing up, vegetables had their place, particularly for company. They were separated in individual "side" dishes or on the plate—green beans in a clump, potatoes in another, with the obligatory meat in another. In fact, the only vegetables that were mixed were carrots and peas, a dreadful frozen or canned combination, served unseasoned and unloved from the pot.

Like so many culinary clichés, all that has gone by the by. I hark back to genteel Southern meals, where a variety of vegetables, sometimes seasoned with a bit of meat, were always present at a family supper. Now I may combine several vegetable and grain dishes for a snappy meal and no one misses the main course at all! I have no compunctions about using leftover vegetables. The microwave and the modern no-stick skillet have made reheating them a breeze. And the wealth of oils, vinegars, and condiments on the market guarantees endless, different ways to present them, either hot or cold.

I also combine leftover cooked vegetables and grains like rice or couscous and reheat them with butter and some herbs or a flavored oil to make a completely different dish. I sometimes add grilled meats or leftovers (taking care that they have been refrigerated properly). In fact, I often try to cook twice as much as I need so that I have something left over to fashion anew to provide a fresh-looking and -tasting side dish in just minutes.

My grocery store sells a wide variety of ready-to-use vegetables—washed broccoli and spinach, julienned broccoli stems and carrots, chopped and jarred garlic, all of which shave precious minutes off the dinner schedule. Do be aware, however, that this convenience can compromise the nutritional value of these foods; if you buy precut greens or vegetables, read the pull dates on the labels, choose the freshest packages, and use as soon as possible—preferably within a day or two.

When I was a young woman I thought everything had to be done at the same time and so I waited until the last minute to cook the vegetables. Now I know that not only vegetables but also potatoes, rice, and other grains can usually be reheated in the microwave or oven, particularly if slightly undercooked. So if dinner is scallopini or quick-cooking meat, I get my sides cooked first, so that everything is hot at the same time.

ASPARAGUS IN VINAIGRETTE

I love asparagus for parties and covered-dish suppers. Since it is such a rich vegetable, most people will only take three or four spears, so for the price it is actually quite economical when in season. Try to get uniform spears to ensure even cooking.

1 pound asparagus, ends trimmed if
   woody and peeled if too thick

VINAIGRETTE
⅓ cup fresh lemon juice
1 tablespoon Dijon mustard
⅔ cup olive, canola, or vegetable oil

Salt
Freshly ground black pepper
Sugar
2 tablespoons chopped fresh herbs (rosemary, basil, oregano, fennel, thyme,
   parsley)

ASPARAGUS FOR A CROWD
This elegant vegetable is one of the easiest things to fix for a big splash with little effort or money, and can be made up to 3 days ahead of serving. Ten pounds of asparagus will serve at least fifty people. Cook the asparagus in 2-pound batches to ensure even cooking, allowing the water to return to the boil between each batch.

Fill a shallow 12-inch frying pan half full with salted water and bring to the boil. Reduce the heat, add the asparagus, and simmer until the spears are crisp-tender, 3 to 5 minutes. While the asparagus cooks, fill the sink with very cold water. Plunge the asparagus into the cold water to stop the cooking and then drain. The asparagus can be refrigerated at this point for 2 to 3 days; bring to room temperature before serving.

In a small mixing bowl, whisk together the lemon juice and Dijon mustard until smooth. In a slow steady stream, whisk in the oil until thick and emulsified. Season to taste with salt, pepper, and sugar. Stir in the chopped herbs. The vinaigrette can be made ahead and refrigerated for 5 days.

Just before serving, toss the asparagus with the vinaigrette and serve at room temperature.

Serves 4

BROCCOLI STIR-FRY

The combination of broccoli stir-fried with bell peppers that have turned red on the vine and a Vidalia onion is hard to beat. It was a shocker to me when former president George Bush said he didn't like broccoli, as it is one of the more adaptable vegetables, taking on the personality of its companions easily. In this case, it's coated lightly with a hot oil and finished off with soy sauce and vinegar, a blend that pairs well with grills or fish. It may be made ahead and reheated.

2 tablespoons olive oil
2 teaspoons chili oil
2 red bell peppers, seeded and cut in
  2-inch wedges
1 large onion, cut in 2-inch wedges

1 head broccoli, florets only (reserve the
  stems for another use)
1 tablespoon soy sauce
1 tablespoon rice wine vinegar
Freshly ground black pepper

Heat the olive oil and chili oil in a wok or skillet until hot. Add the red peppers and onion and stir-fry quickly for about 1 to 2 minutes. Add the broccoli florets and sauté 4 to 5 minutes longer. Add the soy sauce, vinegar, and pepper to taste, toss to combine, and cover to steam lightly until the broccoli is just done, about 3 minutes. Serve immediately.

Serves 6

ZESTY GRATED CARROTS

Grating the carrots in the food processor really speeds up the preparation time for this eye-pleasing side dish. The ginger adds a little zip, but you can use fresh herbs such as marjoram or oregano in place of the ginger. Leftovers can be stirred into a pasta or rice salad; add raisins or serve on a soft lettuce leaf.

1 tablespoon butter
1 to 2 tablespoons chopped ginger or
  ¼ teaspoon grated nutmeg

6 carrots, peeled and grated
Salt
Freshly ground black pepper

Melt the butter in a large skillet over medium-high heat. Add the ginger and grated carrots and cook, stirring constantly, until the carrots are tender and have lost their raw taste, 3 to 5 minutes. Season to taste with salt and pepper.

Serves 4

CELERY AND WALNUTS

This refreshing side dish can become a lunch dish with the addition of drained tuna fish, shrimp, or cooked and slivered chicken. You need blanch the celery only if it is tough.

6 to 8 celery stalks
1 tablespoon soy sauce
1 tablespoon rice or white wine vinegar

⅛ teaspoon Oriental sesame oil
Sugar
½ cup coarsely chopped walnuts

Remove the leaves and tough ends of the celery, and string if necessary. Slice on the diagonal. If the celery is large and tough, drop the slices into a pot of boiling water, return just to the boil, and drain. In a small bowl mix together the soy sauce, vinegar, sesame oil, and sugar to taste. Combine the walnuts with the celery in a large bowl. Pour the sauce over; toss well to combine. Serve warm, at room temperature, or chilled.

Serves 4 to 6

Minted Hot Cucumbers

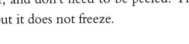

Few people think of cucumbers as a vegetable to serve warm, but delicious minted cucumbers are a natural with fish and a cooling counterpart to curries. They require only a quick sautéing to wilt them, so they're great last-minute fare. I prefer the English or gourmet cucumbers because they contain fewer seeds, have a milder flavor, and don't need to be peeled. This dish can be reheated in the microwave, but it does not freeze.

2 large English cucumbers	*3 tablespoons chopped fresh mint*
1 to 2 tablespoons butter	*Salt*
1 medium onion, chopped	*Freshly ground black pepper*

Cut the cucumbers in half lengthwise and scoop out the seeds with a spoon. Cut in thin slices.

Melt the butter in a skillet over medium heat. Add the onion and sauté until soft. Add the cucumber slices and toss just until tender, about 2 minutes; do not overcook or they will be mushy. Remove from the heat and stir in the mint. Season to taste with salt and pepper and serve immediately.

Serves 4

Variation: Substitute 2 10-ounce boxes of frozen tiny peas (thawed) for the cucumbers and you have a side dish sophisticated enough for roast lamb or chicken.

PEAS AND TOMATO

Colorful and tasty, this side dish is a snap to throw together and an excellent use for fresh or canned tomatoes. Baby lima beans or delicate white acre peas would be pleasing substitutes for the green peas.

1 tablespoon butter
½ 16-ounce package frozen green peas,
  defrosted
1 tomato, cut into ½-inch cubes

1 tablespoon finely chopped fresh basil
Salt
Freshly ground black pepper

Heat the butter in a large skillet over medium heat. Add the peas, tomato, and basil and toss just until warmed through; do not cook too long or the tomatoes will wilt and give up their juices, making the dish too soggy. Season to taste with salt and pepper.

Serves 2 to 3

TOMATO TIPS
To cut a fresh tomato:
Place stem end down on a cutting board. Cut the tomato in a crisscross pattern. Place the tomato on its side and cut downward toward the board. This method of cutting will produce an even result without crushing the tomato. You may core the tomato before you start.

FLASH-FRIED SPINACH

Amazingly, 3 pounds of spinach will cook down to only about 2 cups. The crinkly spinach has more bulk and may yield more than 2 cups. The garlic adds a nice zing to this fast, tangy side dish. The spinach can also be used as a colorful bed for the Grilled Chicken Breasts (page 74). It does not freeze or reheat well, but it can be served at room temperature.

3 pounds spinach, well washed and
  stems removed, or 2 10-ounce pack-
  ages frozen, thawed and squeezed dry
1 to 2 tablespoons peanut oil
6 garlic cloves, peeled and chopped

¼ cup fresh or canned chicken stock or
  broth
1 teaspoon salt
1 tablespoon sesame seeds

SPINACH SENSE
Although fresh spinach cooks in next to no time, it takes more people time to prep than other longer-cooking vegetables. Do not even consider taking short cuts on the rinsing/ draining/rinsing again process; your finished dish will be full of grit and inedible. Instead, wash and trim the spinach the night before, or buy pre-washed spinach in cellophane packages.

Tear the spinach into bite-size pieces. Heat a wok or skillet with the oil. Add the garlic and stir-fry until light brown, about 2 minutes. Add the spinach and stir-fry 1 minute. Stir in the chicken stock and salt and cook 1 minute longer. Sprinkle with the sesame seeds before serving.

Serves 4 to 6

QUICK SQUASH SAUTÉ

A bowl heaped with these yellow and green rounds, layered with slightly brown crunchy onions, is a treat for the eye as well as the palate. For a different look, cut the squashes into $\frac{1}{2} \times 3$-inch fingers.

1 tablespoon olive oil
1 small onion, sliced thickly
1 garlic clove, peeled and chopped
$\frac{1}{2}$ jalapeño pepper, seeded and chopped
1 to 2 yellow squash, cut in $\frac{1}{2}$-inch slices

1 to 2 zucchini, cut in $\frac{1}{2}$-inch slices
Salt
Freshly ground black pepper
2 tablespoons chopped fresh basil
$\frac{1}{2}$ cup grated imported Parmesan cheese

Heat the olive oil in a large skillet. Add the onion, garlic, jalapeño, yellow squash, zucchini, and salt and pepper to taste. Sauté until the vegetables are tender and just beginning to brown, about 10 minutes. Add the basil and cook 1 minute more. Remove from the heat and stir in the Parmesan cheese.

Serves 4

Variation: Sprinkle with feta cheese and black olives and omit the Parmesan cheese for a Mediterranean flavor.

BAKED ROSEMARY SQUASH

This is the perfect accompaniment to pork chops and it requires next to no effort on the part of the cook. It's a really nice side dish when you are too busy to cook.

6 yellow squash, sliced into 1-inch
   rounds
3 tablespoons olive oil
3 tablespoons slightly crushed fresh
   rosemary

1 garlic clove, peeled and finely chopped
Salt
Freshly ground black pepper

Preheat the oven to 350°F.

In a large bowl or resealable plastic bag, combine the squash, olive oil, rosemary, garlic, and salt and pepper to taste. Stir or shake well to coat the squash evenly with oil and seasonings. Spread the squash on a large baking sheet and cook until tender but still slightly crunchy, 20 to 25 minutes.

Serves 4 to 6

GRILLED ZUCCHINI

All of the ingredients for this extremely simple dish are available well into fall, bringing a welcome reminder of the farmer's market to the table. If you cannot grill the squash, broil them in your oven about 2 to 3 minutes per side, or just until the squash begins to brown. For added color, use half yellow and half zucchini squash.

4 to 5 zucchini, cut lengthwise in
   ¼-inch slices
1 red bell pepper, seeded and cut lengthwise in 2-inch wedges
1 tablespoon olive oil
1 tablespoon sherry vinegar or red wine
   vinegar

1½ teaspoons chopped fresh fennel
1½ teaspoons chopped fresh basil
¼ cup shaved imported Parmesan cheese
Salt
Freshly ground black pepper

Prepare the grill or preheat the broiler.

Brush the sliced squash and red pepper with the oil. Grill or broil about 4 minutes per side. Remove to a large bowl and toss with the vinegar, fennel, basil, and Parmesan. Season to taste with salt and pepper and serve warm or at room temperature.

Serves 4 to 6

LAYERED ZUCCHINI AND TOMATOES

This makes a light vegetarian entrée with Spiced Couscous (page 150), a crisp crusty bread, a simple salad, and fresh fruit for dessert, but I love the way it pairs with roast chicken.

3 small zucchini, trimmed and sliced lengthwise into ¼-inch slices
3 tomatoes, sliced and drained on paper towels
Salt
Freshly ground black pepper

1 cup dry breadcrumbs
1 tablespoon chopped fresh oregano
1 cup grated Swiss cheese
1 cup grated imported Parmesan cheese
3 tablespoons butter

Preheat the oven to 400°F. Butter a 9 × 13-inch baking dish.

In the baking dish, layer half the zucchini and then half the tomatoes. Sprinkle with salt and pepper. Mix together the breadcrumbs, oregano, and Swiss and Parmesan cheeses. Sprinkle half over the zucchini and tomatoes. Repeat layering one more time, ending with cheese mixture. Dot with the butter and bake until golden brown and bubbly, 25 to 30 minutes.

Serves 6 to 8

Zucchini and Celery Sauté

This sauté cooks in only 5 minutes and the contrast of the two green colors brightens up any plate. Be sure to have the zucchini and celery cut up before heating the oil and butter. This dish does not freeze well, but can be reheated in 2 to 3 minutes in the microwave.

2 tablespoons olive or vegetable oil

2 tablespoons (¼ stick) butter

4 celery stalks, sliced into ½-inch diagonal slices

6 small zucchini, cut into 1½-inch-long sticks

3 garlic cloves, peeled and chopped

2 tablespoons parsley, chopped

Salt

Freshly ground black pepper

In a large skillet, heat the olive oil and butter until singing. Add the celery slices and sauté for 2 minutes. Add the zucchini sticks and sauté with the celery 2 minutes longer or until crisp-tender. Reduce the heat to medium, add the garlic and parsley, and sauté 1 minute longer. Season to taste with salt and pepper.

Serves 6

ZUCCHINI POINTERS
Zucchini are the chameleons of the garden. They can be eaten raw, steamed, sautéed, grilled, or deep fried and taste completely different each way, so you can serve them as often as you like and never get a complaint! Vary the shape too, cutting them into batons one night, grating and flash-frying them the next. Zucchini are faster to make than frozen peas and stores well for 4 or 5 days in the refrigerator, so be sure to keep them in stock for last-minute dinners.

Julienned Gingered Vegetables

I have become so fond of ginger these days, I frequently "ginger to taste" before I add salt and pepper to taste. It gives these quickly cooked vegetables an extra air of distinction.

2 tablespoons butter or oil

½ to 1 tablespoon finely chopped fresh ginger

2 large carrots (about ½ pound), peeled and julienned (or grated in the food processor)

2 turnips (about ½ pound), peeled and julienned

1 to 2 medium zucchini (about ½ pound), washed and julienned

Salt

Freshly ground black pepper

Heat the butter or oil in a large frying pan until hot. Add the ginger and cook 1 to 2 minutes. Add the carrots and turnips to the ginger and cook 2 to 3 minutes, until just beginning to soften. Add the zucchini and cook 2 to 3 minutes more. Stir to mix well. Season to taste with salt and pepper.

Serves 6

Variation: Replace the ginger with $\frac{1}{2}$ teaspoon ground cumin (or toasted whole cumin seeds) and $\frac{1}{2}$ to 1 teaspoon minced hot pepper. Add 1 teaspoon grated ginger, if desired.

TRICOLOR STIR-FRIED VEGETABLES

Y ou can vary the vegetables every time you make this—just take care to balance colors, textures, and shapes for the most satisfactory result. Tuck leftovers into a burrito with grated cheese or fold into an omelet.

PREP AHEAD
It's a help to take a few hours each week to prepare vegetables for fast cooking later in the week. Vegetables can be washed, and even sliced or chopped, up to 2 or 3 days ahead. This enables you to use a mix of vegetables in several different recipes, giving the illusion of greater variety.

1 tablespoon sesame oil

1 tablespoon soy sauce

3 green onions, sliced

1 garlic clove, peeled and chopped

$\frac{1}{2}$ teaspoon dried hot red pepper flakes

2 medium-large yellow squash, cut in $\frac{1}{4}$-inch slices

$\frac{1}{2}$ pound asparagus, cut diagonally into 2-inch pieces

1 large red bell pepper, seeded and cut into triangles

In a large skillet or wok, heat the sesame oil and soy sauce until very hot. Add the green onions, garlic, and red pepper flakes and cook briefly. Add the squash, asparagus, and bell pepper and cook, stirring constantly, for about 3 minutes. Reduce the heat, cover, and cook for an additional 1 to 2 minutes or until just done—not too soft, not too crunchy.

Serves 4

GREEN BEANS WITH ORANGE VINAIGRETTE

I often make these sweet–sour green beans ahead of time, setting them aside until ready to serve. I can serve them at room temperature or toss them over heat with the orange dressing for a tangy hot side dish. Save leftover vinaigrette to combine with strips of cooked roast beef for a hearty salad or use in a summer pasta with black olives.

2½ pounds young green beans, tipped
   and tailed

ORANGE VINAIGRETTE
½ cup fresh orange juice
Grated peel (no white attached) of 2
   oranges
1 red bell pepper, roasted, peeled, and
   seeded
4 green onions

2 garlic cloves, peeled
2 tablespoons chopped fresh thyme
2 tablespoons coarse-grained Dijon
   mustard
¼ cup red wine vinegar
1 cup peanut oil
Salt
Freshly ground black pepper
Sugar

In a large pot of boiling water over high heat, quickly cook the green beans until just barely tender, 7 to 10 minutes. Drain and rinse with cold water to refresh. May be cooked in advance and refrigerated.

In a food processor, purée the orange juice, peel, red pepper, green onions, garlic, thyme, mustard, and red wine vinegar until smooth. With the processor running add the oil in a thin, steady stream until the dressing is thick and emulsified. Season to taste with salt, pepper, and a pinch of sugar. The dressing can be made ahead and refrigerated for 1 to 2 days. Toss with the blanched beans about 5 minutes before serving, or combine in a skillet and reheat quickly over medium–high heat. Serve warm or at room temperature.

Serves 6 to 8

Basil and Cheese Stuffed Tomatoes

Large Italian tomatoes are not usually as ripe and juicy as those we get in the summer or even our Roma tomatoes, so a not-quite-ripe tomato will do very well for this. Fontina cheese adds a lovely nutty flavor and melts beautifully.

TOMATO TRICKS

To seed a tomato: Cut the tomato in half horizontally, not from stem to blossom end. The seeds will be exposed and can easily be removed by lightly squeezing the tomato or by scooping them out with your finger. If the tomato is particularly juicy, do this over a strainer placed inside a bowl, to catch the juices.

4 medium tomatoes
2 tablespoons chopped fresh parsley
2 tablespoons chopped fresh basil
1 garlic clove, peeled and chopped
¼ cup olive oil
Salt

Freshly ground black pepper
4 slices Fontina or mozzarella cheese

GARNISH
Basil leaves
Parsley sprigs

Preheat the oven to 450°F. Grease an ovenproof casserole.

Slice the stem ends off the tomatoes, and scoop out the inside pulp and seeds. Turn upside down on a rack to drain completely. Mix the parsley, basil, garlic, and oil. Season to taste with salt and pepper. Divide the filling among the tomatoes. Place the tomatoes closely together, but not touching, in the casserole. Bake for about 5 minutes, then top each tomato with a slice of cheese, and return to the oven for another 10 minutes. Serve hot, garnished with basil leaves and parsley sprigs.

Serves 4

Variation: In the summer you may find "roly poly," a baseball-shaped summer squash, at the local farmer's market. Use it instead of a tomato for a change—it will bake in 20 minutes.

Sautéed Mushrooms and Vegetables

Mushrooms marry well with a variety of green vegetables, and they are a good extender for leftover cooked vegetables. You can really change the flavor of this dish by substituting a good-quality peanut, pecan, walnut, or sesame oil for the olive oil.

2 to 4 tablespoons butter

½ pound button mushrooms, cleaned, stems removed, halved

1 to 2 cups sliced cooked vegetables (broccoli, carrots, zucchini, green beans, etc.)

2 cups fresh snow peas

Salt

Freshly ground black pepper

1 tablespoon sesame seeds, preferably black (optional)

Heat the butter in a large skillet over medium-high heat. Add the mushrooms and cook until their liquid has almost evaporated and they're beginning to brown, 3 to 5 minutes. Add the cooked vegetables and the snow peas and heat through, 2 to 3 minutes. Season to taste with salt and pepper and top with the sesame seeds if using.

Serves 4

CLEANING MUSHROOMS

Place in a colander and spray briefly with water. Dry the mushrooms quickly with a tea towel. Remove the stems only if brown. Alternately, place in a large plastic bag with 2 tablespoons flour, fill the bag ¾ full with cold water, and shake quickly several times. Pour off the water. The grit leaves with the flour and water.

Spinach Sauce

Even as a child I loved soothing, homey creamed spinach, which inspired this verdant multipurpose sauce. Use it as a bed for grilled fish or to top baked potatoes. For company meals, the addition of cream makes this an elegant last-minute sauce, but, for every day, try the yogurt instead. Leave the frozen spinach in the refrigerator in the morning so it will be defrosted by dinner time.

2 10-ounce boxes frozen chopped spinach, thawed
1 tablespoon butter
1 medium onion, finely chopped

½ teaspoon freshly grated nutmeg
1 cup heavy cream or plain yogurt
Salt
Freshly ground black pepper

Squeeze the spinach to remove excess moisture. In a large skillet, melt the butter on low heat. Add the onion and cook until soft and translucent, 3 to 4 minutes. Add the spinach and nutmeg, and simmer for 5 minutes. Transfer the solids to a food processor and purée until smooth. Return the purée to the skillet and stir in the cream or yogurt. Bring to a gentle simmering boil, add salt and pepper to taste, and serve hot.

Makes 3 cups

GARLIC ROASTED POTATOES

While a baked potato can take as long as an hour to cook, halved new potatoes the size of a golf ball cook in about half the time. These potatoes are mahogany brown and crispy. Leftovers reheat well enough for another meal.

1 pound small new potatoes, well scrubbed and halved
4 garlic cloves, peeled and coarsely chopped

3 tablespoons olive oil
Salt
Freshly ground black pepper

Preheat the oven to 350°F. Spray a 15 × 10-inch baking sheet with nonstick spray.

In a large bowl, toss the potatoes with the garlic and oil. Season liberally with salt and pepper. Spread the potatoes on the baking sheet, allowing room between them. Bake in the oven, tossing once or twice, until the potatoes are soft in the center and a rich brown on the outside, 25 to 30 minutes.

Serves 4 to 6

Herbed Mashed Potatoes

Herbs add a different twist to this lighter version of mashed potatoes so the heavy cream is not missed. If fresh basil is not available, use 1 to 2 tablespoons of pesto sauce (store-bought is fine) or try substituting other fresh herbs such as thyme or parsley. Cutting the potatoes into ¼-inch cubes reduces the cooking time to only 15 to 20 minutes. The potatoes should be roughly mashed, giving them a "down home" texture.

*2 to 3 pounds all-purpose potatoes,
  peeled and cut into ¼-inch cubes*

1 teaspoon salt

½ cup milk or buttermilk

¼ cup (½ stick) butter

Salt

Freshly ground black pepper

2 tablespoons finely chopped fresh basil

Place the potatoes in a large pan with cold water to cover by an inch. Add the salt and bring them to the boil. Reduce the heat and simmer until soft, about 15 to 20 minutes. Drain well. In a heavy saucepan, heat the milk and butter together until almost boiling.

Return the potatoes to their saucepan over a low heat and mash with a sturdy fork. Add some of the hot milk mixture and blend well. Continue adding the milk mixture until the desired consistency is reached. Stir in the salt, pepper, and chopped basil, and serve immediately.

Serves 4 to 6

POTATO PANCAKES

Chopped bell peppers update a traditional holiday favorite. Actually, since the potatoes cook quickly because they are grated, this makes a nice addition to any meal and should not be relegated to holiday menus exclusively. They are as welcome with eggs for brunch as with a thick, juicy steak for supper!

2 large baking potatoes
1 small onion, chopped
3 tablespoons finely chopped red bell pepper (optional)
1 large egg, lightly beaten

2 tablespoons all-purpose flour
Salt
Freshly ground black pepper
Vegetable or corn oil for frying

Peel the potatoes and grate them, using a hand grater or food processor. Transfer them to a colander and squeeze out the excess liquid. Pat dry with paper towel.

In a mixing bowl, combine the potatoes with the onion, bell pepper, egg, and flour and season to taste with salt and pepper. Blend well.

Pour enough oil into a large skillet to cover the surface and place over medium-high heat until very hot. Drop the batter into the skillet by heaping tablespoonfuls and flatten with the back of the spoon. Cook until the bottoms are golden brown, about 5 minutes. (Tip: If the potatoes resist turning, they may be too thick and thus not cooked through. They will turn easily only when cooked through.) Turn the pancakes and cook the other side until browned, about 3 minutes. Place the finished pancakes in a paper-towel-lined pan and keep warm in a 200°F. oven while you cook the remaining batter. Season with additional salt, if desired, at the last minute.

Serves 4

Scalloped Sweet Potatoes

Fresh sweet potatoes take too long to bake to be considered "fast food," but canned sweet potatoes can be adequate stand-ins if they get some dressing up. This is good enough for Thanksgiving and totes and reheats well.

1 28-ounce can sweet potatoes, drained
1½ cups heavy cream
Salt
⅛ to ¼ teaspoon freshly grated nutmeg

Freshly ground black pepper
¼ cup grated Swiss cheese
¼ cup fine dry breadcrumbs, browned in
   3 tablespoons butter

Preheat the oven to 350° F. Butter a shallow 2½-quart baking dish.

Combine the potatoes and cream in a medium saucepan over medium-high heat. Season to taste with salt, nutmeg, and pepper. Bring to the boil, stirring constantly to prevent scorching.

Pour the potato mixture into the baking dish. Mix together the cheese and breadcrumbs and spread evenly over the top. Bake 25 minutes until browned and bubbling.

Serves 4

SWEET POTATO SHORTCUTS
If you have a real aversion to canned vegetables, it is simple enough to bake 2 small potatoes earlier in the week and reserve them for this dish. Bake the potatoes until cooked, but not mushy, so you can cube them.

Ribboned Potatoes

Some people just don't feel a meal is complete without potatoes, but there isn't always time to bake or boil them for a quick supper. This method of cutting really speeds up the potatoes' cooking time and the ribbons are also pretty. They make an unusual and attractive bed for grilled beef or pork. Buy moist potatoes that feel heavy for their size. The new crop of bakers that comes in in the fall months is exceptionally juicy and flavorful.

4 large baking potatoes, peeled
2 tablespoons butter
2 tablespoons chopped fresh parsley

Salt
Freshly ground black pepper

To make ribbons, pare strips from the potatoes with a vegetable peeler. Drain in a colander.

Heat the butter in a large skillet over medium-high heat. Add the potatoes and cook until tender, about 5 minutes, stirring constantly. Add the chopped parsley, season to taste with salt and pepper, and serve hot.

Serves 4

BULGUR PILAF

Bulgur, cracked wheat that has been precooked and toasted, is now available in so many grocery stores it should be considered for every-day meals. It's almost as fast to cook as couscous and adds a nutty grain flavor and whole-grain nutrition to your meal. Add onion, garlic, carrot, and spices and it moves into the "very special" realm.

1 cup bulgur
1 cup boiling water
1 tablespoon olive oil
1 medium onion, chopped
2 garlic cloves, peeled and finely chopped

1 large carrot, peeled and grated
1½ teaspoons cumin
1 cup fresh or canned chicken stock or broth

Put the bulgur in a medium mixing bowl and cover with the boiling water. Set aside to soften for 10 minutes. Heat the oil in a large skillet or Dutch oven. Add the onion and cook 2 to 3 minutes until softened. Add the garlic and carrot and cook until soft, 3 to 4 minutes. Add the bulgur, cumin, and chicken stock and bring to the boil. Add the bulgur. Cover, reduce the heat, and simmer about 10 minutes, until the liquid is absorbed. Serve hot.

Serves 4 to 6

SPICED COUSCOUS

Couscous is hands down the fastest starch side dish to make. Because I drink so much hot tea, I have an instant hot water dispenser on my sink. I put the couscous in a heatproof measuring cup with the butter and salt, add the piping hot water, cover it with plastic wrap, let it sit for 5 minutes, and fluff it with a fork into a serving dish. Why, I wonder, should I feel guilty when life is so easy?

$2\frac{1}{2}$ cups water or fresh or canned
  chicken stock or broth
$\frac{1}{4}$ cup ($\frac{1}{2}$ stick) butter
Salt (optional)

2 cups quick-cooking couscous
$\frac{1}{4}$ teaspoon ground cinnamon, or to
  taste
$\frac{1}{4}$ teaspoon cayenne pepper, or to taste

In a large saucepan, bring the water or stock to the boil. Add the butter and salt. When the butter has melted, stir in the couscous. Cover, remove the pan from the heat, and let sit 5 minutes. Fluff with a fork and season to taste with the cinnamon and cayenne pepper.

Serves 4 to 6

Variation: Lemon Couscous—Add grated peel (no white attached) and juice of 4 lemons to the water. Omit the butter and salt. Just before serving add 6 chopped green onions and 2 tablespoons finely chopped fresh basil in place of the cinnamon and cayenne.

FRIED RICE

REHEATING RICE

It's just as easy to cook 2 cups of rice as it is to cook one, so I always make a double batch to ensure leftovers, which I'll reheat later in the week. Refresh cold rice in a colander placed over steaming water for 5 or 10 minutes, or add a bit of water, cover tightly, and microwave on high for about 1½ to 2 minutes.

Sometimes I'll serve this as a whole meal; other times, it's a side dish for an Asian one. When I was a child my mother took us to a local Chinese restaurant once a month as a treat. Maybe that's why I still love fried rice and order it out in Chinese restaurants as well as make it at home. It's a great place to use leftover rice. To enhance this dish, try shiitake mushrooms in place of regular button mushrooms.

1 to 2 tablespoons peanut oil

1 cup mushrooms, sliced

4 cups cooked rice, preferably made with
   chicken stock

½ teaspoon sugar

1 teaspoon dry sherry (optional)

1 tablespoon soy sauce

2 eggs, beaten

1 cup chopped red leaf or romaine lettuce

GARNISH

3 green onions, finely chopped, green
   and white parts

Heat the oil in a large skillet over high heat. Add the mushrooms and sauté for 1 to 2 minutes to coat and start cooking. Add the cooked rice and stir-fry until the rice is heated and the oil is evenly distributed. In a small bowl, combine the sugar, sherry if using, and soy sauce. Add to the rice and mix well. Stir in the eggs and blend well. Add the lettuce and cook, stirring 1 minute longer. Garnish with the green onions.

Serves 4 to 6

Baked Mushroom Rice

Leftover sautéed mushrooms were the inspiration for this hearty side dish when I discovered a container in the fridge that was not enough to "do anything with." This doubles easily, freezes, and reheats well.

1 tablespoon butter
½ medium onion, chopped
1½ cups long-grain white rice
2¼ cups water

½ tablespoon salt
½ pound small button mushrooms,
  quartered
Freshly ground black pepper

Preheat the oven to 350°F.

In an ovenproof pot, heat the butter over medium heat. Add the onion and cook until soft and slightly brown, 5 to 7 minutes. Add the rice and stir well to coat with the butter. Add the water and salt and bring to the boil. Stir in the mushrooms and cover with a tight-fitting lid. Bake for 17 minutes. Fluff with a fork, pepper to taste, and serve.

Serves 4 to 6

NOTE: *This can also be prepared on top of the stove. Bring to the boil after adding the mushrooms, then cover, reduce the heat to a low simmer, and cook for 17 minutes.*

RUSH-HOUR RICE

I've made my peace with many convenience foods and shortcut products, but instant rice is one that has never made much sense to me. It's a rare occasion when I can get dinner on the table in less than the 20 minutes or so it takes to boil or bake long-grain rice, and once it's at a low simmer or in the oven it doesn't require any watching. Instant rice offers negligible advantages and has a far less appealing texture.

Dried Fruit–Nut Muffins ■ *Peanut Butter and Banana Muffins* ■ *Salsa Corn Bread* ■ *Currant and Cranberry Scones* ■ *Sesame Bread Sticks* ■ *Beer Corn Bread Muffins* ■

7 BREADS

Olive-Rosemary Focaccia ■ *Thyme and Cheese Biscuits* ■ *Biscuit Mix with Three Cheeses* ■ *Squash and Carrot Nut Bread* ■ *Oregano French Loaf* ■ *Banana Bread* ■ *Virginia's Loaf Bread*

DESCENDED AS I AM from generations of bakers, I am grateful that many of the store-bought breads now available rival those my grandmother baked each week. But, fresh, hot home-baked breads make a meal. And while rush hour dinners certainly don't accommodate the luxury of twice-risen yeast breads, there are ways to short cut the process enough to make it feasible even for weeknights. In this I've included quick breads—usually leavened with baking powder or baking soda—as well as several yeast breads that use the microwave method to speed the rising time and a no-knead variety.

Planning also helps fit bread baking into a busy schedule. I find that I can start a yeast bread first thing, which only takes a few minutes, let it rise while I'm getting organized and cooking my meal, and by the end of dinner it has risen, ready for baking and reheating another day or for freezing. Or, I start the bread as I cook, let it rise overnight in the refrigerator, and bake it the next day.

Flatter and smaller breads such as focaccia take less time both in rising and baking than loaf breads, as do rolls and small loaves. Rolls and small loaves are more quickly baked. (If you're cooking for a crowd, however, the shaping becomes time-consuming, and a loaf would in the long run take less of your attention, even though it takes longer to rise and bake.)

Muffins and quick breads are among the best options for those of us who grew up eating homemade bread at every meal. Usually they take less time to assemble, and require no rising time.

Preheating the oven the second you have a chance speeds all baking on its way, and starting it before you move on to the rest of the meal helps considerably. I find I can frequently bake my dessert and my bread at the same temperature, baking them simultaneously if there is room in the oven for the air to circulate around them.

There are very few quick breads that don't freeze well, and most make enough for you to have several meals' worth if carefully wrapped and reheated. The variety of breads offered in restaurant baskets allows us to mix as if it was planned, so there is no longer pressure to have a quantity of any one bread.

DRIED FRUIT–NUT MUFFINS

These are really tasty muffins to have on hand for breakfast or snacking. Don't bother worrying about the kind of fruit. Use the mixed bits or whatever you have on hand.

2 eggs
1 cup packed dark brown sugar
2 cups all-purpose flour
1½ teaspoons baking powder
1 teaspoon baking soda
Pinch of salt
1 tablespoon vegetable oil

1 cup orange juice
¾ cup chopped dried fruit, any combination
¾ cup chopped almonds
2½ tablespoons finely chopped orange peel (no white attached)

STORING DRIED FRUIT
Most dried fruits will not spoil when stored at room temperature. Dates, however, have more moisture and should be refrigerated after opening. Do store dried fruits in an airtight, resealable container to prevent them from drying out too much and getting hard. If your dried fruit does turn hard, plump in hot water for a few minutes, or heat for a few seconds with water in the microwave oven.

Preheat the oven to 350°F. Grease muffin tins.

In a mixer, combine the eggs and sugar and beat at high speed until the mixture is light in color and forms a ribbon when the beaters are lifted. Sift together the flour, baking powder, baking soda, and salt. In a mixing cup, whisk together the vegetable oil and orange juice. Stir the dry ingredients into the egg-sugar mixture in thirds, alternating with the orange juice and beginning and ending with the dry ingredients. Fold in the chopped dried fruit, almonds, and orange peel.

Pour the batter into the prepared muffin cups about two-thirds full. Bake 20 minutes or until a wooden skewer inserted near the center comes out clean. Cool briefly in the pan on a rack, then remove the muffins from the tin and cool on a rack.

Makes approximately 18 muffins

Peanut Butter and Banana Muffins

You'll find lots of reasons to make these muffins. I take them to baseball games, serve them at tea time—and kids love them any time. They do look a little sunken in the middle when done but are so moist and delicious I don't mind. The muffins are a good use for "nearly over-the-hill" bananas and they freeze well up to 4 months.

2½ cups all-purpose flour
2 teaspoons baking powder
1 teaspoon baking soda
½ teaspoon salt
½ cup (1 stick) butter, softened
½ cup packed light brown sugar
½ cup granulated sugar

3 eggs, lightly beaten
½ cup buttermilk
2 large very ripe bananas, mashed
  (about 1 cup)
½ cup crunchy peanut butter
2 teaspoons vanilla extract
¼ cup chopped peanuts

Preheat the oven to 350°F. Grease and flour 3 6-cup muffin tins or use cupcake liners.

Sift together the flour, baking powder, baking soda, and salt. In a mixing bowl, beat the butter with the sugars until light, about 2 minutes. Add the eggs and buttermilk to the sugar mixture and mix well. Add the bananas, peanut butter, and vanilla and mix thoroughly. Gently stir in the flour mixture until just combined. Pour into the prepared muffin tins, filling about two-thirds full. Top with the chopped peanuts, pressing lightly into the batter. Bake until a toothpick inserted in the center comes out clean, about 15 to 20 minutes. Remove from the oven. Allow to sit 5 minutes, loosen the sides with a knife or spatula, then invert onto a cooling rack to cool completely.

Makes 18 muffins

SALSA CORN BREAD

Good-quality jarred salsa, either tomatillo or tomato, adds a distinctive Southwestern flair to a traditional corn bread recipe, although if you have homemade on hand it would certainly be just as good. The corn bread is good crumbled over hearty soups or chili, and it can be made as muffins for a more dressed-up affair. It freezes for 2 months and reheats, thawed and wrapped in foil, 15 minutes at 350°F.

2 tablespoons peanut oil
2 cups cornmeal (see Note)
1 cup all-purpose flour (see Note)
1 tablespoon baking powder
1 teaspoon baking soda
1 teaspoon salt

1 egg
1½ cups buttermilk
1 cup Tomatillo Salsa (page 29) or
   tomato salsa
1 teaspoon black pepper or to taste

Preheat the oven to 425°F. Pour the peanut oil into a 10-inch ovenproof skillet and put into the oven until very hot.

Meanwhile, in a large bowl, mix together the cornmeal, flour, baking powder, baking soda, and salt. Add the egg, buttermilk, and the hot oil from the skillet and combine thoroughly. Stir in the salsa and pepper and combine with a few quick strokes. Pour the mixture into the hot skillet and bake 20 to 24 minutes, or until the corn bread is a nice golden brown. Remove from the oven, cool briefly on a rack, invert, and turn out of the pan. Cut into wedges to serve.

Serves 8

NOTE: *If using self-rising flour, omit the baking soda, baking powder, and salt. You may also use 3 cups of self-rising cornmeal in place of the cornmeal, flour, baking powder, baking soda, and salt.*

Variation: For a Savory Blue Cheese Corn Bread, substitute ¾ cup crumbled blue cheese for the salsa and the black pepper.

CURRANT AND CRANBERRY SCONES

Scones are delicious for afternoon teas but can quickly become stale. Fortunately, it is a simple matter to bake them up as needed when the dough is partially prepared. You'll be able to treat guests to the delicious aroma of baking scones with only a few last minute steps. This can be frozen for up to 3 months.

3 cups self-rising flour
1/4 cup sugar
1/2 teaspoon baking soda
1/2 teaspoon salt
1 teaspoon ground coriander
5 tablespoons butter, chilled
1 cup buttermilk

1 egg, lightly beaten
1/2 cup currants
1/2 cup dried cranberries

GLAZE
1 egg beaten with 1 tablespoon milk
1 tablespoon sugar

Preheat the oven to 475°F. Lightly grease a 10 × 13-inch baking sheet.

In a large bowl, sift together 2½ cups of the flour, the sugar, baking soda, salt, and coriander. With a pastry cutter, two knives, or your fingers, cut in the chilled butter until the mixture resembles coarse meal. This may be done several days in advance.

Make a well in the center of the flour mixture and add the buttermilk and egg. Lightly stir together until the flour is moistened and you have a very wet dough. Add the currants and cranberries and mix just until they are evenly distributed throughout the dough. Sprinkle the remaining ½ cup of flour over the dough and turn in the bowl until the dough has an even coating of flour.

With floured hands, pinch off pieces of the dough and roll gently between your palms so the entire surface is coated with flour. Lightly flatten into 2-inch circles about ½ inch thick and place on the baking sheet just barely touching.

If desired, brush the scones with the glaze. Sprinkle the scones with the sugar. Bake until golden brown, 10 to 12 minutes. Serve immediately.

Makes 12 scones

SESAME BREAD STICKS

Two kinds of sesame seeds add interest to these quick-to-make sticks. Serve with drinks or dinner. The quick-rising yeast enables you to skip the first rising, although I find there is much more flavor when they get both risings. If you don't have time to shape all the dough into sticks, the remaining dough can wait, refrigerated and covered, for a day or two, or be baked as a focaccia in the 10 × 14-inch rectangle, for 20 to 30 mintues.

1 package quick-rising yeast
1/2 teaspoon salt
2 to 3 cups bread flour
1/2 cup hot milk (130°F.)
1/4 cup water
1 tablespoon honey
1 tablespoon softened butter

G L A Z E   A N D   T O P P I N G
1 egg yolk, mixed with 2 tablespoons
   water
1/2 tablespoon white sesame seeds
1/2 tablespoon black sesame seeds

Preheat the oven to 375°F. Grease 2 baking sheets.

In a food processor or a mixer, pulse the yeast, salt, and 2½ cups flour until lightly mixed. Add the milk, water, honey, and butter. Process, adding flour as needed, until the dough is smooth and elastic, about 1 minute. Make a hole in the center of the dough to create a large doughnut. Place in a lightly greased microwave-safe bowl and cover with a damp cloth. Place a microwave-safe cup of water in the back corner of the microwave. Place the covered dough in the microwave. At 10 percent power, heat 3 minutes, then let rest for 3 minutes. Repeat. Then, heat for 3 minutes and let rest 6 minutes. The dough should be doubled in bulk. (This step may be omitted.)

Punch the dough down and roll out on a floured surface until you have a rectangle ¼ inch thick and approximately 10 × 14 inches. Cut into 10 × ½-inch strips. Roll each strip into a stick. Let double. Place on the baking sheets, ¾ inch apart. Brush with the egg glaze and sprinkle with the mixed sesame seeds. Place the sheets immediately into the oven and bake 12 to 15 minutes, until light golden brown. Remove from the oven and cool on a rack. The sticks freeze well.

Makes 28

Variation 1: Sprinkle coarse salt on the sticks along with the sesame seeds before baking, or just salt alone.

Variation 2: Focaccia—Punch the dough down, place in a greased 10 × 14-inch baking sheet or jelly roll pan, and press the dough out ¼ inch thick. Let double, brush with egg glaze, and sprinkle with mixed sesame seeds. Bake in the oven at 375°F. until light brown, 12 to 15 minutes. Remove and cool on a rack.

BEER CORN BREAD MUFFINS

SELF-RISING FLOUR
An old-fashioned convenience food, self-rising flour eliminates the need to measure out baking powder and salt for sweet and savory baking recipes. The real time savings are admittedly negligible, but some days every minute counts! To make your own, add 1 tablespoon of baking powder and 1 teaspoon of salt to every 2 cups of all-purpose flour. Be sure to use very fresh baking powder if you will be storing your self-rising flour for any period of time, and keep tightly covered.

Teaming the sweet, salty taste of beer with cornmeal and cheddar cheese makes for a hearty, savory muffin. Serve them with soup or chili or a spicy summer grill of bratwurst. These muffins freeze for 2 to 3 months tightly wrapped.

2 cups white or yellow cornmeal
1 cup self-rising flour (or 1 cup all-purpose flour plus 1½ teaspoons baking powder and ½ teaspoon salt)
1 tablespoon baking powder
1 teaspoon salt

1 tablespoon sugar (optional)
¼ cup (½ stick) butter, melted
2 eggs, beaten
8 ounces beer or nonalcoholic beer
½ cup buttermilk
1 cup shredded cheddar cheese

Preheat the oven to 400°F. Grease a 12-cup muffin tin. Set aside.

Sift together the cornmeal, flour, baking powder, salt, and sugar, if using. In a large bowl, mix together the melted butter, eggs, beer, buttermilk, and cheese. Add the sifted dry ingredients and stir until just combined. Divide the batter among the 12 muffin cups, filling each cup about two-thirds full. Bake 20 to 25 minutes or until they are light golden brown and a wooden skewer inserted near the center comes out clean. Cool in the tins on a wire rack.

Makes 12 muffins

OLIVE-ROSEMARY FOCACCIA

This puffy, Italian-inspired flatbread (also called *schiacciata* or *fugazza*) is topped with herb-flavored pools of oil. It is wonderful as an appetizer, a quick lunch with a green salad, or a sandwich bread. If you are in a rush, you can omit the first rising, although the focaccia will not be as light; just move straight to shaping the dough. I bake it in a rectangle on a baking sheet, but if you want to use a pizza tin and make it round, that's just fine. When made in a food processor, the olives and herbs in the dough give an interesting variegated look.

2½ to 3 cups bread flour
1 package quick-rising yeast
2 teaspoons sugar
1 teaspoon salt
¼ cup hot water (130°F.)
¾ cup milk, at room temperature
¼ cup olive oil
2 tablespoons chopped fresh rosemary

½ cup black olives, preferably Greek or
    Italian, drained, pitted, and chopped
1 tablespoon cornmeal

T O P P I N G
¼ cup olive oil, preferably herb flavored
½ cup chopped olives
¾ cup grated imported Parmesan cheese

Preheat the oven to 375°F. Grease a baking sheet and sprinkle with cornmeal.

In the food processor, combine 2 cups of the flour, the yeast, sugar, and salt. Add the water and olive oil, and process until smooth. Add the remaining flour, ½ cup at a time, to make a soft dough. Turn out onto a floured board and knead in the rosemary and olives until smooth and elastic.

With your thumbs, punch a hole in the dough to form into a doughnut shape and place it in a microwave-safe mixing bowl. Cover loosely with a damp tea towel and place in the microwave. Place a microwave-safe glass of water in the back of the microwave. Heat at 10 percent power for 3 minutes. Let rest for 3 minutes. Repeat. Heat for 3 minutes and let rest for 6 minutes, or until doubled in bulk.

When doubled, punch down and knead briefly on a floured board. When the dough is smooth, roll it out into a 10 X 13-inch rectangle. Transfer to the prepared baking sheet. Let rise again until doubled, about 20 minutes.

When doubled, press lightly several times with your fingers to make indentations in the dough. Brush or drizzle lightly with the olive oil and sprinkle with the chopped olives and Parmesan cheese. Place in the preheated oven and bake until golden, 25 to 30 minutes. Remove to a wire rack to cool. Serve warm or at room temperature.

Variation: Replace the rosemary with 2 tablespoons of chopped basil, increase the salt by 1 tablespoon, and replace the olives with ⅓ cup chopped sun-dried tomatoes.

Makes 1 flatbread

THYME AND CHEESE BISCUITS

You'll love this flavorful and unusual variation on the beloved Southern biscuit. For variety, substitute basil, rosemary, or oregano for the thyme, or experiment with your favorite herb.

FAST BUTTERMILK
If you don't regularly keep fresh buttermilk on hand, you can whip up a very satisfactory substitute in just seconds: 1 teaspoon of lemon juice will "sour" a cup of regular milk, imparting a tang similar to buttermilk's. Or, look into stocking powdered buttermilk, which is reconstituted with water and works especially well in baking recipes.

4 cups self-rising flour (page 161)
2 teaspoons salt
2 tablespoons finely chopped fresh thyme

6 tablespoons shortening
1¾ cups buttermilk
½ cup grated cheddar cheese

Preheat the oven to 500°F. Grease a baking sheet.

Sift 3 cups of the flour and the salt together into a bowl. Add the thyme. Cut in the shortening with a pastry blender or a fork until the mixture resembles coarse meal. Add the buttermilk and mix until the dough holds together; it will be wet and sticky. Mix in the cheese.

Put the remaining cup of flour in another bowl. Flour your hands and then pull off a golf-ball-size piece of dough. Roll the piece of dough lightly in the flour to coat on all sides. Roll it gently into a smooth ball in the palm of your hand. This kneads the dough as well as smoothes and shapes it.

Place the biscuits, barely touching each other, on the pan and flatten slightly. Bake 8 to 10 minutes on the top rack or until golden brown. Serve hot.

Makes 20

BISCUIT MIX WITH THREE CHEESES

Stir up a batch of this homemade convenience product when you have a few extra minutes; fresh hot biscuits with a savory tang of cheese will be just 15 minutes away. The mix can be refrigerated for up to a month, and you can use as much or as little of the mix at a time as you like; just use one part milk or buttermilk for every two parts biscuit mix.

BISCUIT MIX
11 cups self-rising flour (page 161)
2 teaspoons salt
1 tablespoon coarsely ground pepper
(optional)
½ cup chilled butter
½ cup chilled shortening

1 cup shredded cheddar cheese
½ cup shredded Swiss or Monterey Jack cheese
½ cup grated imported Parmesan cheese

1 cup milk or buttermilk
1 cup all-purpose flour, approximately

In a large mixing bowl, whisk together the self-rising flour, salt, and pepper, if using. With two knives or a pastry cutter, cut in the butter and shortening, then add the cheeses and continue to work into the flour. Place in an airtight container and store in the refrigerator.

To use, preheat the oven to 500°F. Gently combine the milk or buttermilk with 2 cups of mix until just blended. Pull off biscuit-size hunks of dough, dip in the flour, and pat into a smooth ball. Flatten slightly and place, sides touching, in an ungreased cake pan. Bake until golden brown, 8 to 10 minutes.

Makes approximately 60 biscuits

SQUASH AND CARROT NUT BREAD

This bread has a pleasant taste full of fresh flavor with a slight crunch from the carrots and pecans, and it's not too sweet. Grate the squash, carrots, and orange peel and chop the pecans a day ahead, so that you can combine everything when you get in; it will be ready to eat in just over half an hour. If you prefer, the batter can be baked in one 9 × 5 × 3-inch pan for about 55 minutes. The bread freezes for 2 to 3 months.

2 yellow squash, grated
2 carrots, peeled and grated
¾ cup chopped pecans
½ cup sugar
2 tablespoons grated orange peel (no
   white attached)

½ cup (1 stick) melted butter or
   vegetable oil
½ cup lowfat plain yogurt
2 eggs, beaten
1¾ cups self-rising flour (page 161)
½ teaspoon ground coriander
Pinch of nutmeg

Preheat the oven to 350°F. Grease and flour two 7 × 3 × 2-inch loaf pans. Cut a piece of wax paper to fit the bottom of each pan and grease and flour the paper.

In a large bowl, mix together the squash, carrots, pecans, sugar, and orange peel. In another bowl, combine the butter, yogurt, and eggs. Sift together the flour, coriander, and nutmeg. Stir the egg mixture into the flour and mix well. Fold in the squash and carrot mixture and stir until just combined. Pour the batter into the prepared pans and bake 35 to 40 minutes until golden and a toothpick inserted in the center comes out clean. Cool for 10 minutes on a rack and then remove the breads from the pans and cool on a rack.

Makes 2 loaves

OREGANO FRENCH LOAF

The technique of using the microwave to speed up the rising time for breads is especially effective when you use it for the second rising. If you use a microwave-safe glass loaf pan you can force a second rising in the microwave as well. Do keep in mind that these shortcut bread recipes will work perfectly well with traditional rising methods if you have the time. If so, you should use a traditional baguette pan rather than microwave-safe loaf pan.

1 package quick-rising yeast
2½ to 3½ cups bread flour
1 teaspoon salt
1½ teaspoons sugar

2 tablespoons finely chopped fresh
* oregano*
1 cup hot water (130°F.)

Preheat the oven to 400°F. Grease a microwave-safe 8½ × 4½-inch loaf pan.

In the food processor or mixer, combine the yeast, 2½ cups of the flour, the salt, sugar, and oregano. Add the water and process to make a soft dough, adding some of the remaining flour if needed.

Form the dough into a ball. With your thumbs, punch a hole in the dough to form into a doughnut shape and place it in a microwave-safe mixing bowl. Place a microwave-safe cup of water in the back of the microwave. Cover the dough loosely with a damp tea towel and place in the microwave. Heat at 10 percent power for 3 minutes. Let rest for 3 minutes. Repeat. Finally, microwave for 3 minutes and let rest for 6 minutes, or until doubled in bulk.

Turn the dough onto a floured board and punch down. Knead and shape into an oblong the length of the pan. Place in the prepared pan and push down with your fingers to fill up the pan.

If using a glass pan, return the dough in the pan to the microwave and repeat the microrising process. Alternatively, cover with a damp towel and set in a warm spot to rise until doubled. Place the risen loaf on the middle rack of the oven. Bake until the internal temperature registers 200°F. on an instant-read thermometer, 20 to 25 minutes. Remove the loaf from the pan and let cool on a rack.

Makes 1 loaf

BREAD PAN SIZES
"Quick bread" is something of a misnomer, for although they don't require the long rising times of yeast breads, quick breads are generally quite dense and need as much as 50 minutes to an hour to bake. You can significantly shorten the baking time of any quick bread by making it into mini-loaves, using two or three 7 × 3 × 2-inch bread pans. Reduce the total baking time by 15 to 20 minutes, rearranging the loaves once during baking.

BANANA BREAD

Dark and delicious, this bread is just sweet enough for dessert, and really nice for an afternoon or evening snack. Use bananas that are too soft to eat; the skins should be well spotted with brown and very soft.

5 to 6 overripe bananas
1 cup packed light brown sugar
1 cup granulated sugar
4 eggs, slightly beaten
½ cup (1 stick) butter, softened

1 cup chopped pecans
2½ cups all-purpose flour
1 teaspoon salt
2 teaspoons baking soda

Preheat the oven to 350°F. Grease a 9 × 13-inch baking pan.

In a mixing bowl, mash the bananas with a wooden spoon or the paddle attachment of your mixer. (You should have about 2½ cups.) Add the brown sugar, sugar, eggs, butter, and pecans and blend well. On a sheet of wax paper, sift together the flour, salt, and baking soda. Add the dry ingredients to the banana mixture. Continue mixing until all the ingredients are well blended. Pour the batter into the prepared pan. Bake 25 to 30 minutes until a knife inserted into the bread comes out clean.

Makes 24 squares

VIRGINIA'S LOAF BREAD

This recipe is adapted from Bernard Clayton's *New Complete Book of Breads*. My most recent kitchen director was Virginia Willis, and she could not resist working with this recipe, which was originally entitled Sister Virginia's Daily Loaf. It is slightly richer than a French loaf, made with milk, shortening, and a little sugar. It can be doubled.

1 package quick-rising yeast
3 cups bread flour
1 teaspoon salt
1 tablespoon sugar
½ cup hot water (130°F.)
½ cup milk

1 tablespoon vegetable shortening

GLAZE
1 egg mixed with 1 tablespoon water
Pinch of salt

Preheat the oven to 350°F. Grease a 9 × 5-inch loaf pan.

In the mixer or food processor, mix together the yeast, 2 cups of the flour, salt, and sugar. Add the water, milk, and shortening. Combine well. Add the remaining flour ½ cup at a time as needed. Knead in the food processor about 1 minute or with the dough hook of a mixer for 10 minutes until soft, smooth, and elastic.

Form the dough into a ball. With your thumbs, punch a hole to form into a doughnut shape and place it in a microwave-safe mixing bowl. Place a microwave-safe cup of water in the back of the microwave. Cover the dough loosely with a damp tea towel and heat at 10 percent power for 3 minutes. Let rest for 3 minutes. Microwave a second time for 3 minutes and let rest for 6 minutes, or until doubled in bulk.

Place on a floured board and shape the dough into a loaf. Place in the prepared pan. If the pan is glass, cover and repeat the microrise process. If metal, let rise until double at room temperature.

Brush the top of the loaf with the egg glaze. Place the pan into the oven and bake until a rich golden brown and a quick-read thermometer registers 200°F., 35 to 40 minutes. Turn the loaf onto a wire rack to cool.

Makes 1 loaf

Baby Apple Crumb Cakes ∎ *Quick Chocolate Cake* ∎ *Ray's Ginger Brownies* ∎ *Quick Cake Brownies* ∎ *Chocolate Raspberry Won Ton Packets* ∎ *Raisin Gingerbread Cakes* ∎ *Quick Pineapple Cake* ∎ *Chocolate Raspberry Cobbler Cake* ∎ *Crisp Apple Cobbler* ∎ *Chocolate Oatmeal Bars* ∎ *Almond Chocolate Bars* ∎ *Nutty Toffee Bars* ∎ *Grandmother's Danish Cookies* ∎ *Applecream and Cookies* ∎ *Sugar and Spice Squares* ∎ *Broiled Tropical Fruit* ∎ *Berry Gratin* ∎ *Bananas Foster*

DESSERTS

∎ *Strawberries with Balsamic Vinegar* ∎ *Plum or Fruit Caramel Pudding* ∎ *Panna Cotta* ∎ *Shortcut Floating Islands* ∎ *Chocolate Truffle Squares* ∎ *Mini Chocolate Fudge Drops* ∎ *Peach, Pear, or Plum Brûlée* ∎ *Quick Rice Pudding* ∎ *Peach Fool* ∎ *Baked Pineapple Alaska* ∎ *Caramelized Pears and Apples* ∎ *Chocolate-Dipped Fruit* ∎ *Orange Flummery* ∎ *Beginner's One-Crust Pie Dough* ∎ *Blueberry Pie* ∎ *Rustic Apple Half-Pie* ∎ *Maple Yogurt Sauce* ∎ *Raspberry-Lemon Cheese Pie*

MY SWEET TOOTH grows stronger each year, with a particular leaning toward chocolate, fruit, and caramel. Time has never been crucial when it comes to sweets—thinking about them, planning them is often part of the pleasure. This anticipation also eases the pressure a bit when I have to rush home and put a meal together in a hurry. I must think "what's for dessert" before I start preparing the main course. Is it already made or must I make it? Then I can arrange my dessert preparations.

Here is a case where speed of cooking is less important than speed of preparation. An easily assembled cake or cobbler can bake for an hour while you eat and then be served with the after-dinner coffee with no more fuss. And throughout dinner the delicious aromas wafting from the kitchen as it bakes gives the diners a hint of the pleasures still to come. It is important in these cases, however, to be sure that the dessert is actually in the oven rather than languishing on the counter due to lack of organization.

Alternatively, there are desserts that require last-minute cooking. If the oven or broiler is necessary it should be preheating during dinner, if it wasn't already used for another part of the meal. Then, you should at least clear a preparation space so it's possible to run in and throw it together. It's best to clear off dishes and pots and pans so the diners can come in and visit and will not see the cook and the kitchen in disarray. This time before dessert is frequently the most conversational part of the evening, and leaving the table for an extended period gives the cook a feeling of missing out on something.

Of course, not all of the dessert needs to be prepared by the cook. There are wonderful store-bought ice creams and cookies, for instance, to provide good company for desserts that need a little extra. If you want to make your own accompaniments, remember that bar cookies are much easier on your time than drop cookies. It may take longer to bake a pan of bar cookies, but there is only one pan, not a series of them going in and out of the oven.

Whatever route you take, a glorious dessert is part of the magic of dinner. I urge you to take the few moments necessary to assemble one and leave your family and friends with the satisfied feeling that only decadence can inspire.

BABY APPLE CRUMB CAKES

These soft cinnamon and apple delights, with a crumbly topping reminiscent of Dutch apple pie, are very tasty. When they are served, particularly to young women, I frequently hear, "How cute! This reminds me of my mother's cakes, so buttery and cinnamony." High praise to my ears. The cakes may also be made ahead several days or frozen.

TOPPING
½ cup (1 stick) butter
1 cup all-purpose flour
½ cup rolled oats
¾ cup sugar
1½ to 2 teaspoons ground cinnamon

BATTER
1½ cups all-purpose flour
¾ cup whole wheat flour
1 cup sugar

1 tablespoon baking powder
1 teaspoon ground cinnamon
¾ cup (1½ sticks) butter, melted
⅓ cup milk
3 eggs, lightly beaten
1 teaspoon vanilla extract
2 Granny Smith apples, peeled and
   coarsely chopped
½ cup raisins
½ cup chopped pecans

Preheat the oven to 350°F. Grease and flour a 12-cup muffin pan and set aside.

In a small bowl, combine the butter, flour, oats, sugar, and cinnamon with your fingers until the mixture forms crumbs. Set aside.

In a large bowl sift together the all-purpose and whole wheat flours, sugar, baking powder, and cinnamon. Add the melted butter, milk, eggs, and vanilla and beat with a wooden spoon just until the batter is blended; do not overbeat. Gently fold in the apples, raisins, and pecans.

Spoon the batter into the prepared muffin pan and then sprinkle the crumbs over the tops, pressing gently. Bake until the tops are golden and springy to the touch and the crumbs are crisp, about 30 minutes. Cool in the pans on a wire rack for 5 minutes. Carefully unmold and serve warm or at room temperature.

Makes 12 muffins

QUICK CHOCOLATE CAKE

T his recipe is an adaptation from *Le Chocolat*, a wonderful book about chocolate by Martine Jolly. The really great trick to this dessert is that it can be made ahead and eaten at room temperature or, better yet, can be put together and baked while you eat supper! Serve with a dollop of whipped cream and chocolate shavings.

OVEN IDIOSYNCRA-SIES

Learn about your oven. If its thermostat is not accurate, it may be slowing you down—or burning your food. Buy an oven thermometer and check your thermostat at several different temperatures. When you feel confident about your oven temperature, you can experiment with higher temperatures on your favorite recipes. Try a dish you used to cook at 350° at 375°F. You may shave a good deal of time off the final result with no penalty. If a short cooking time doesn't give a sufficiently browned result, consider a quick broil at the end.

¼ cup water

1 12-ounce package semisweet chocolate chips

½ cup (1 stick) butter, cut into cubes and softened

4 eggs, separated

1 tablespoon all-purpose flour

1 tablespoon sugar

1 teaspoon vanilla

Pinch of cream of tartar

GARNISH

Whipped cream

Chocolate shavings

Preheat the oven to 300°F. Grease and flour an 8 × 12-inch pan.

Combine the water and chocolate chips in a medium-size saucepan and melt over low heat. Remove from the heat and beat in the butter piece by piece. Stir in the egg yolks one at a time. Add the flour, sugar, and vanilla.

In a separate bowl, beat the egg whites and cream of tartar to form stiff shiny peaks. Whisk a bit of the egg whites into the chocolate mixture to lighten, then fold the chocolate into the whites. Pour the batter into the prepared pan and bake for 20 minutes; the cake will seem slightly undercooked. Cool on a wire rack, then invert onto a cake plate and cut into squares. Serve each square with a dollop of whipped cream and sprinkle with chocolate shavings.

Serves 8

RAY'S GINGER BROWNIES

These brownies have very little batter and are just bursting with nuts and chocolate—how bad can that be? The ginger adds a sweet hotness that complements the chocolate flavors.

½ cup (1 stick) butter, softened
1 cup packed light brown sugar
1 egg, lightly beaten
1 tablespoon rum
1 teaspoon vanilla extract
½ teaspoon almond extract

⅓ cup cocoa
⅔ cup all-purpose flour
½ teaspoon salt
1½ cups chopped pecans
½ cup semisweet chocolate chips
1 tablespoon chopped candied ginger

Preheat the oven to 325°F. Grease and flour a 9-inch square baking pan.
In a medium bowl, beat together the butter, sugar, egg, rum, vanilla, and almond extract until light, about 5 minutes. Sift together the cocoa, flour, and salt and combine with the butter mixture, stirring just until mixed. Fold in the pecans, chocolate chips, and ginger. Pour the batter into the pan and bake 25 to 30 minutes. Do not overbake. Cool in the pan on a wire rack, then cut into squares.

Serves 8 to 10

A WORD ON MIXES

Why buy a mix when you've got most of the ingredients on hand already? Actually, there are good reasons to rely on mixes occasionally. I have found them very handy for weekends in a vacation cabin when I knew I couldn't use up a large bag of flour or cornmeal. And mixes can be purchased in small, individual-use packets that keep them pest-free and more easily portable. Those I've found most handy are biscuit, corn bread, muffin, and brownie mixes. However, I usually do add things to them to make them my own: peppers to the corn bread mix, cheese to the biscuits, nuts to the brownies, and blueberries to the muffins. Nonetheless, I'm often grateful for the service they provide.

QUICK CAKE BROWNIES

Mixed and baked in the same pan, these fudgy squares are an absolute lifesaver when you need a quick dessert. They also have less fat than many brownie recipes.

1½ cups all-purpose flour
1 cup sugar
¼ cup cocoa
1 tablespoon baking powder
Pinch of salt

½ cup (1 stick) butter, melted
1 tablespoon vanilla extract
1 tablespoon apple cider vinegar
1 cup cold water

Preheat the oven to 350°F.

Sift together the flour, sugar, cocoa, baking powder, and salt into a 9-inch square baking pan. Add the butter, vanilla extract, vinegar, and water to the dry ingredients and stir well until blended. Bake until a knife comes out clean, 30 to 35 minutes. Invert onto a rack to cool, then cut into squares.

Serves 8 to 10

CHOCOLATE RASPBERRY WON TON PACKETS

When dazzle is imperative, take Chocolate Truffle Squares and pop them inside won tons with raspberries and fry until crisp. You may assemble the won tons ahead of time and even freeze them before frying (don't defrost, but do watch for splatters). I suggest you make 2 for each guest, then assemble the rest later and freeze them for another occasion.

½ package won ton wrappers
⅓ recipe Chocolate Truffle Squares
  (page 190)
½ pint fresh raspberries
⅓ cup raspberry jam

1 cup peanut oil
½ pint vanilla ice cream
½ cup good store-bought chocolate sauce
  (optional)

Move a won ton to a piece of wax paper. Place 1 teaspoon of the chocolate mixture in the center, and add 3 or 4 raspberries and ¼ teaspoon raspberry jam. Brush the outside edge with water, fold the won ton corner to corner, with all 4 corners meeting in the center, and press lightly to seal. Alternatively, fold in a flat triangle. When you have 4 done, heat the peanut oil in a heavy sauté pan or cast-iron skillet. Add the won tons and fry until crisp, turning as necessary. Drain on paper towels. Repeat with the next 4 won tons.

Meanwhile, put a scoop of ice cream in each of 4 stemmed glasses. Add 2 won tons, and drizzle with chocolate sauce, if using. Top with another raspberry or two.

Serves 4

RAISIN GINGERBREAD CAKES

Candied ginger is a worthwhile addition to any baker's pantry, and once you become accustomed to having it around, you'll find numerous uses for it. Just one tablespoon makes these adult cupcakes sublime. Serve with the very simple, but truly delicious, Lemon Yogurt Cheese Sauce. The muffins freeze well for about 3 months, but when you have half an hour to make them while everything else is cooking, try them for a last-minute dessert to round out a lighter meal. The sauce can be refrigerated for 1 week. The muffin by itself could be a sweet bread that is particularly nice with a stew, but I serve them primarily as a dessert.

2 tablespoons rum, light or dark according to your taste
1 tablespoon chopped candied ginger
1 cup raisins
2½ cups self-rising flour (page 161)
2 teaspoons ground ginger
1 teaspoon ground cinnamon
1 teaspoon ground coriander
½ cup packed light brown sugar
½ cup molasses
½ cup (1 stick) butter, softened

2 eggs
1 teaspoon vanilla extract

LEMON YOGURT CHEESE SAUCE

1 cup yogurt cheese (see sidebar)
½ cup confectioners' sugar
2 tablespoons lemon juice
1 tablespoon grated lemon peel (no white attached)
1 teaspoon vanilla extract

Preheat the oven to 375°F. Grease and flour a 12-cup muffin tin and set aside.

In a small bowl, toss the rum with the candied ginger and raisins. Sift together the flour, ginger, cinnamon, and coriander. In a large bowl beat together the brown sugar, molasses, and butter with an electric mixer until light, about 2 minutes. Add the eggs and vanilla and beat 1 minute more. Stir in the flour mixture and mix until just blended. Fold in the candied ginger, raisins, and rum.

Fill the muffin tins about two-thirds full and bake about 25 minutes. Remove the muffins from the oven, cool for 5 minutes in the pan, then remove from the pan, and cool completely on wire racks.

While the muffins cool, make the Lemon Yogurt Cheese Sauce: In a small bowl combine the yogurt cheese, confectioners' sugar, lemon juice, lemon peel, and vanilla until smooth. Serve the cooled muffins with a dollop of sauce.

Makes 12 muffins

QUICK PINEAPPLE CAKE

This cobbler-style cake is a real winner when time is of the essence. Use apples or pears if pineapple is unavailable, although canned pineapple makes an acceptable substitute for fresh. Many stores sell pineapple already peeled and cored, making your job easier.

*1 pineapple, peeled, cored, and cut into
  1-inch chunks*
1 tablespoon lemon juice
1 cup packed brown sugar, light or dark
½ teaspoon ground cinnamon
½ cup (1 stick) butter, melted

2 eggs, lightly beaten
¼ cup sour cream
1 teaspoon vanilla extract
1 cup all-purpose flour
1 tablespoon granulated sugar

Preheat the oven to 350° F. Lightly butter a 9 × 12-inch baking pan.

In a medium-size bowl, toss together the pineapple, lemon juice, ¼ cup of the brown sugar, and cinnamon. Pour into the prepared baking dish. In another bowl, mix together the butter, the remaining ¾ cup of brown sugar, eggs, sour cream, and vanilla until just blended. Fold in the flour and spread the batter evenly over the pineapple. Sprinkle with the granulated sugar and bake the cake until the top is golden and crusty around the edges, about 30 minutes. Cool slightly on a wire rack before cutting into squares and serving.

Serves 8

CHOCOLATE RASPBERRY COBBLER CAKE

This simple "throw together" recipe bakes to a rich golden brown with bits of the chocolate melted throughout the raspberry-dotted batter; it always causes a sensation whenever I serve it. You can use frozen raspberries; just cut down on the sugar accordingly if they are presweetened. The cobbler freezes up to 2 months.

QUICKER COBBLERS
If you have self-rising flour (page 161) you can make super-simple cobblers and crisps. The easiest recipe yet is 1 cup self-rising flour, 1 cup sugar, 1 cup milk, ⅛ cup melted butter, and 2 cups fruit (fresh or frozen). Mix together and bake in a 9 × 13-inch pan at 350° F. for 30 minutes. So delicious!

¾ cup (1½ sticks) unsalted butter

2 cups all-purpose flour

2 teaspoons baking powder

½ teaspoon salt

1½ cups milk

1 teaspoon vanilla extract

1½ cups firmly packed light brown sugar

4 cups raspberries

1 cup semi-sweet chocolate chunks

Preheat the oven to 350° F.

Melt the butter in a 9 × 13-inch baking dish. In a large bowl, mix together the flour, baking powder, salt, milk, vanilla, and brown sugar. Pour half of the batter directly into the hot, buttered pan. Add 3 cups of the raspberries and the chocolate chunks. Pour the remaining batter over the berries, then top with the last cup of berries. Place the pan in the oven and bake 35 to 40 minutes or until the center is set. Let cool at least 10 minutes before serving.

Serves 6 to 8

CRISP APPLE COBBLER

I've taught a simple cobbler, an old-time Southern favorite, for years. This crispy version is enriched with raisins.

5 medium Golden Delicious apples

½ cup raisins or currants

1 cup granulated or packed brown sugar

½ cup (1 stick) butter

1 cup all-purpose flour

1½ teaspoons baking powder

½ teaspoon salt

1 cup milk

Preheat the oven to 375°F.

Peel and core the apples and slice ½-inch thick (you should have about 3 cups). In a mixing bowl, toss the apples, raisins, and sugar. Put the butter in an 9 × 13-inch ovenproof serving dish and place in the oven to melt. Sift the flour, baking powder, and salt together in a bowl. Stir in the milk to make a batter. Pull the hot dish of melted butter out of the oven and pour in the batter, which will bubble around the sides. Quickly spoon the apples evenly over the batter. Return to the oven and bake until the dough is brown and has risen up around the fruit, about 25 to 30 minutes. Serve with Maple Yogurt Sauce (page 198).

Serves 6 to 8

CHOCOLATE OATMEAL BARS

Oats and whole wheat flour give this rich, indulgent bar cookie an appealing texture not found in plain brownies and bar cookies. The pecans could easily be replaced with walnuts or almonds, as you like.

1 cup butter, softened
¾ cup packed dark brown sugar
1 egg, lightly beaten
1½ teaspoons vanilla extract
1 cup rolled oats

1 cup pecans, finely chopped
½ cup whole wheat flour
½ cup all-purpose flour
1 cup semisweet chocolate chips

Preheat the oven to 350°F. Grease a 9 × 13-inch baking pan.

In a mixer, cream together the butter and sugar until light. Add the egg and vanilla. On low speed, add the oats, pecans, whole wheat flour, and all-purpose flour. Stir in the chocolate chips.

Spread the dough in the prepared pan. Bake until light golden brown, 20 to 25 minutes. Cool on a wire rack and cut into squares.

Makes 24

ALMOND CHOCOLATE BARS

This cookie has the fastest and easiest homemade type of crust, which can also be used for pies. It requires no prebaking and a food processor speeds it up considerably. Wonderfully buttery and sweet, these delights are addictive! If you use self-rising flour (page 161) in place of the all-purpose flour, omit the baking powder and salt.

CRUST
1 cup all-purpose flour
¼ cup packed light brown sugar
½ cup (1 stick) butter, softened
1 teaspoon almond extract
1 teaspoon vanilla extract

ALMOND FILLING
½ cup (1 stick) butter, melted
1½ cups packed light brown sugar

1 egg, lightly beaten
2 teaspoons vanilla extract
1¼ cups all-purpose flour
1 teaspoon baking powder
Pinch of salt
1½ cups chopped almonds
1 cup semisweet chocolate chips

Confectioners' sugar

Preheat the oven to 350°F. Lightly grease and flour a 9 × 13-inch baking pan.

To make the crust, in a food processor, combine the flour, sugar, butter, almond extract, and vanilla extract. The mixture should be crumbly. Press evenly into the baking dish.

Using the same food processor bowl to make the filling, combine the butter and sugar. Add the egg and vanilla and pulse. Add the flour, baking powder, and salt and process until smooth. Quickly pulse in the almonds and chocolate chips. Spread the almond mixture onto the crust. Bake 20 minutes until golden brown. Remove from the oven and cool on a rack. Sprinkle with confectioners' sugar and cut into bars.

Makes 24

Nutty Toffee Bars

These simple-to-prepare cookies are a real delight, and baking the batter in a single pan saves the time of dropping the cookies individually. A simple frosting is made by sprinkling chocolate chips on the warm cookies and spreading it thin when melted. Heath bits seem to be most available at holiday time. These freeze for 3 months.

1 cup (2 sticks) butter, softened
1 cup packed light or dark brown sugar
1 egg
1 teaspoon almond extract
2 cups all-purpose flour
¾ cup whole almonds
½ cup semisweet chocolate chips

½ cup Heath bits or semisweet chocolate chips

T O P P I N G
¾ cup semisweet chocolate chips
½ cup Heath bits or semisweet chocolate chips

Preheat the oven to 350°F. Lightly spray a 15 × 10 × 2-inch jelly roll pan. Set aside.

In the bowl of an electric mixer, beat together the butter and brown sugar until light. Add the egg and almond extract and beat until well combined, about 1 minute. Add the flour, almonds, chocolate chips, and Heath bits and stir until well combined. Press into the prepared pan. Bake until golden, about 20 to 25 minutes. Remove from the oven and immediately sprinkle with the chocolate chips. After 5 minutes, spread the chocolate smoothly over the top with a small spatula. Sprinkle with the Heath bits, allow to cool, and then cut into squares.

Makes 48

GRANDMOTHER'S DANISH COOKIES

Sometimes there's nothing better with good strong coffee or a glass of milk than a straightforward, unadorned sugar cookie. When they're this easy to make, why not treat yourself on the spur of the moment?

½ cup shortening
½ cup (1 stick) butter, softened
1 cup sugar
1 teaspoon vanilla extract
1 egg, lightly beaten

2 cups all-purpose flour
½ teaspoon baking soda
½ teaspoon cream of tartar

2 tablespoons confectioners' sugar

Preheat the oven to 350°F.

In a mixing bowl, cream the shortening, butter, sugar, and vanilla until light. Beat in the egg. Sift together the flour, baking soda, and cream of tartar and add to the butter mixture. Mix until well blended.

Drop the dough by the teaspoonful about 2 inches apart on an ungreased cookie sheet. Dip the bottom of a small glass or ⅓-cup metal measuring cup into the confectioners' sugar and use it to flatten the tops of the cookies. Bake until the edges are light brown, 8 to 10 minutes.

Makes 3½ dozen

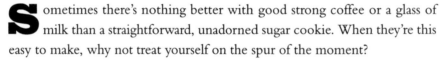

SHORTENING VERSUS BUTTER

I don't have great luck softening butter in the microwave, so if I haven't remembered to leave the butter out in advance, I look for a recipe that uses shortening rather than butter. In fact shortening can often replace butter in cookie recipes; aside from the flavor differences, shortening makes a somewhat softer, loftier cookie, while butter-based cookies are crisper.

APPLECREAM AND COOKIES

This is a ridiculously simple dessert, so easy it is almost like cheating! It's the perfect solution if you are between a rock and a hard place and need something sweet and fast with a hint of sophistication.

1 cup heavy cream

1 tablespoon confectioners' sugar

1 cup applesauce

1 teaspoon candied ginger, finely
   chopped

4 to 8 cookies of your choice

In a food processor or mixer, whip the heavy cream to soft peaks. Gently fold in the sugar, applesauce, and candied ginger. Serve in individual bowls and accompany with the cookies.

Serves 4

SUGAR AND SPICE SQUARES

Even without a drop of butter, these wonderfully rich and spicy little squares deliver a wallop of flavor, thanks to a heady blend of spices and rum flavoring. They can be thrown together in the food processor in about 5 minutes.

1 cup sugar

¾ cup all-purpose flour

1 teaspoon baking powder

1 teaspoon cinnamon

½ teaspoon freshly grated nutmeg

¼ teaspoon ground cloves

¼ teaspoon ground ginger

1 cup dates, chopped

1 cup almonds, chopped

2 eggs, lightly beaten

1½ teaspoons rum extract

Preheat the oven to 350° F. Grease and flour a 9-inch square cake pan.

In a food processor or mixer, blend together the sugar, flour, baking powder, cinnamon, nutmeg, cloves, and ginger. Quickly pulse in the dates, almonds, eggs, and rum extract. Pour the batter into the prepared pan and bake for 25 to 30 minutes. Remove to a rack to cool slightly. Cut into 1½-inch squares and serve warm.

Makes 36

BROILED TROPICAL FRUIT

Bananas Foster (see opposite) inspired this dessert, which is significantly lower in fat than the original recipe. Even if the fruit is not perfectly ripe, it will be nicely flavored by the caramelized brown sugar. A dollop of vanilla frozen yogurt is a nice addition if you want to keep the calorie count low; otherwise, serve with ice cream or a bit of heavy cream.

1 pineapple, peeled, cored, and cut into
   1-inch chunks
2 bananas, peeled and cut into 1-inch
   chunks
¼ cup flaked unsweetened coconut
¼ cup sliced almonds

¼ cup packed brown sugar, light or dark
½ teaspoon ground cinnamon
Grated peel (no white attached) of 1
   orange
2 tablespoons rum or 1 teaspoon rum
   extract
2 tablespoons orange juice

Preheat the broiler.

In a medium-size bowl, combine the pineapple, bananas, coconut, sliced almonds, brown sugar, cinnamon, orange peel, rum, and orange juice. Toss to coat completely. Pour into a shallow broilerproof dish and broil 4 to 6 inches from the heat until the sugar and juices begin to caramelize, about 3 to 4 minutes. Serve hot or at room temperature.

Serves 4

BERRY GRATIN

It used to be that good strawberries were available only in the summer. (When I lived in England, good strawberries were synonymous with Ascot and Wimbledon.) Now berries from Florida, California, and other points south make desserts like this possible all year round.

Make this dessert at the last minute, or combine the berries with the optional liquors before the meal and add the whipped cream mixture just before broiling.

NO-BRAINER FRUIT DESSERTS

Fresh fruit, perhaps served with a bit of cheese, is the very epitome of a no-fuss dessert. If you feel you *must* serve something a bit more "done," try one of these:

• Thread chunks of pineapple, strawberries, bananas, peaches, or nectarines on wooden skewers and grill
• Toss cubed fruits with a tropical juice blend and flaked coconut for easy ambrosia
• Whirl 1 cup of frozen blueberries or strawberries with vanilla yogurt and serve in tall glasses
• Macerate a mix of summer berries with thin strips of orange peel, a tablespoon of sugar, and ¼ cup Grand Marnier to serve over pound cake
• Top wedges of cantaloupe with vanilla yogurt and fresh blueberries
• Serve ripe figs with a dollop of sweetened ricotta cheese
• Sprinkle peach halves with brown sugar and broil until browned

1 cup ripe strawberries, quartered

1 cup fresh raspberries

1 tablespoon Chambord, Framboise, or
   fresh orange juice

1/4 cup heavy cream

2 large egg yolks

1/4 cup confectioners' sugar

2 to 3 teaspoons finely grated orange
   peel (no white attached)

Fresh mint leaves for garnish

Preheat the broiler.

Mix the berries and liquid, and place in an 8-inch shallow gratin dish. Whip the cream until thick. Whisk the egg yolks until thick and pale yellow. Fold in the whipped cream, sugar, and orange peel. Pour over the berries. Place the gratin dish 6 inches from the heat until the top is lightly caramelized, 3 to 4 minutes. Garnish with mint and serve right away.

Serves 4

BANANAS FOSTER

Brennan's Restaurant in New Orleans was the birthplace of this classic dessert. I've devised a really quick and simple version that is made with ingredients that are always on hand. It really shines when served with vanilla ice cream; the warm butter-sugar melts the ice cream and makes pools of irresistible goodness.

1/2 cup (1 stick) butter

1/2 cup packed dark brown sugar

4 bananas, peeled and cut in half
   lengthwise

1/2 teaspoon ground cinnamon

1/2 teaspoon freshly grated nutmeg

1/2 cup heavy cream

1 pint vanilla ice cream

In a large skillet over medium-high heat, melt the butter and sugar together until the sugar dissolves. Add the bananas, cinnamon, and nutmeg, reduce the heat, and cook the bananas 3 to 5 minutes on each side. Stir in the cream and simmer 2 to 3 minutes until thickened.

Put a scoop of ice cream in each dessert dish. Top with 2 banana halves and drizzle with the pan juices.

Serves 4

Strawberries with Balsamic Vinegar

Balsamic vinegar is produced in the Italian provinces of Modena and Reggio from the musk of the Trebbiano grape. It is aged in kegs for a minimum of 12 years and really superior vinegars are aged up to 50 years. I was fortunate enough to have an opportunity to sample a gold-seal balsamic vinegar and meet the slender, patrician woman whose family had made this vinegar with reverence for many generations. Like honey, it was smooth and soothing to the throat.

Although I have one bottle of gold-labeled balsamic (and one of silver, of slightly lesser quality), I usually use a regional, commercial vinegar that costs a fraction of the good stuff. But in a simple dish like this one, use the best balsamic vinegar you can afford.

6 cups strawberries, hulled and halved	1 to 2 tablespoons sugar (depends on the
Grated peel (no white attached) of 1	sweetness of your berries)
lime	
1 teaspoon freshly ground black pepper	GARNISH
6 tablespoons balsamic vinegar	Lemon balm sprigs (optional)

In a glass bowl, combine the strawberries, lime peel, black pepper, balsamic vinegar, and sugar. Toss well and let sit for 10 minutes. Before serving, garnish with lemon balm sprigs, if desired.

Serves 6 to 8

LEMON BALM
This lemony-flavored herb grows like mint—in other words, like a weed. It multiplies year after year in a sunny, moist spot, providing a constant supply for your kitchen.

But its lemon flavor is fleeting and disappears in baked goods, unlike the sturdier lemon flavor of another herb, lemon verbena. So reserve lemon balm for garnishes or herbal teas, where the flavor is dissolved in hot water, then iced. When using as a garnish, bruise the leaves to bring out their wonderful fragrance.

PLUM OR FRUIT CARAMEL PUDDING

I've made this recipe with the tiny fresh plums that grow outside my office window in Oxford, Mississippi. It is so delicious that way I wish they were available year round, but when they are not, I use berries or canned plums. This may be served hot or cold.

1½ cups packed brown sugar, light or dark

4 to 6 slices of good-quality bread, white, whole wheat, or brown, crusts removed

2 pounds ripe plums, halved and stoned, or 1 16-ounce can of plums, or 1 pound berries

2 to 4 tablespoons butter

2 cups vanilla ice cream or whipped cream

Preheat the oven to 350°F.

Thickly butter the sides and bottom of an 8-inch pie dish or other oven-proof dish and sprinkle with some of the sugar. Line the dish with one-third of the bread. Place a layer of the plums, cut side up, or berries on top of the bread. Sprinkle with more sugar. Cover with another layer of bread and a second layer of plums and sugar. Butter the remaining bread and place, buttered side up, on top of the plums. Cover with a round of parchment paper. Bake 30 minutes, remove the paper, and bake 5 to 10 minutes longer, until the fruit is cooked and juices extruded. Serve with ice cream or whipped cream.

Serves 4

Panna Cotta

I first fell in love with this luxurious, luscious dessert in a renowned restaurant in Parma, the home of rich cream. Now I see it prominently placed on the dessert menus of fine restaurants. No wonder. It seems quite light and is very refreshing. Everyone will take second helpings and beg for the recipe. It can stand alone but it is particularly pretty with a spoonful of sweetened, puréed berries. If you have a bit of time, the uncooled mixture can be poured into the mold and refrigerated until set, 4 to 6 hours, rather than stirred over ice.

2½ cups heavy cream
¼ cup sugar, or more to taste
Vanilla bean, split, or ½ teaspoon
  vanilla extract

2 teaspoons powdered gelatin
  (1 package)
¼ cup cold water
½ cup sweetened berries (optional)

Oil a 3½-cup mold or shallow soufflé dish.

Heat 1 cup of the cream with the sugar and vanilla bean until small bubbles form on the sides, 2 to 3 mintues. Remove from the heat and remove the bean. (If using vanilla extract, add it now.) Meanwhile, sprinkle the gelatin over cold water in a small metal cup or pan and let it develop into a sponge. Melt the gelatin over gentle heat. Stir the dissolved gelatin into the warm cream, then stir in the cold cream. Place over a pan of ice and stir until nearly set. Pour into the prepared mold. Refrigerate ½ hour or until completely set.

Gently pull the dessert away from the edge of the mold to "catch an air bubble." Put an oiled serving plate on the mold and turn over. Give the mold a shake to unmold the panna cotta onto the plate.

Serve with the berries, if desired.

Serves 4

SHORTCUT FLOATING ISLANDS

Traditionally, floating islands are cooked in a hot liquid on top of the stove, cooled on paper towel, and placed on top of a cold custard, and then garnished with spun sugar. This recipe saves a few steps by baking the eggs in the custard until slightly caramelized. It may be served right from the oven, and you may choose any number of finishes to give it the final pizzazz. Some ground caramel or nut brittle would be a wonderful alternative to the chocolate or orange rind. Vanilla beans leave charming black specks that really add to the dish.

4 egg yolks
½ cup sugar
Pinch of salt
2 cups milk
1 vanilla bean, split, or 1½ teaspoons
   vanilla extract
3 egg whites

GARNISH
1 tablespoon grated chocolate or orange
   peel (no white attached) (optional)
½ cup fresh berries (optional)

Preheat the oven to 475°F.

Lightly mix the egg yolks and 3 tablespoons of the sugar with the salt. Meanwhile, heat the milk with the vanilla bean in a very heavy pot. When small bubbles form around the edge of the pan, stir some of the hot milk into the lightly mixed yolks, and then return the whole mixture to the pan. Cook over low heat 5 to 10 minutes until the mixture thickens and reaches 180°F. or leaves a small separation in the sauce on the back of a metal spoon. Remove the vanilla bean. If using vanilla extract, add it now.

Pour the custard into a 5 × 10-inch heatproof dish and set aside. Beat the egg whites until stiff. Fold in the rest of the sugar. Spoon small mounds of the meringue onto the custard. Place in the hot oven for 2 to 3 minutes until the meringue colors slightly and becomes crisp. Sprinkle with the chocolate, orange rind, or berries if using. Serve right away or chill and serve cold.

Serves 4 to 6

Chocolate Truffle Squares

Shaping truffles takes time, but no one will snub these easily cut and served squares, believe you me!

1 cup finely chopped pecans, walnuts, or
   pistachios
1 cup heavy cream

12 ounces semisweet chocolate chips or
   good-quality chocolate bar

   Line an 8-inch square pan with wax paper leaving 2 inches of paper overhanging two opposite sides. Sprinkle half the nuts on the wax paper.
   Heat the cream in a heavy saucepan. Add the chocolate and stir until it is melted. (Alternatively, melt the chocolate separately in the microwave and then combine with the cream.) Gently pour over the nuts. Top with the remaining ½ cup of the nuts, pressing them in. Put in the freezer until hard, about 30 minutes. Pull up the wax paper and turn upside down onto another piece of paper using the wax paper to help. Remove the wax paper and cut into 1-inch squares.

Makes 64

Mini Chocolate Fudge Drops

This is a drop version of my pantry fudge, made with fat-free sweetened condensed milk. Dropping the candy is *much* easier than rolling them by hand. Use pretty little candy or mini muffin liners for a snazzier presentation. When Eagle introduced the first fat-free sweetened condensed skimmed milk in 1995, I switched all of my recipes. Why add unnecessary fat when it tastes as good and is fast?

2 6-ounce packages semisweet chocolate chips (2 cups)

6 1-ounce squares unsweetened baking chocolate

1 14-ounce can Eagle Brand fat-free sweetened condensed skimmed milk

1 tablespoon grated orange rind (no white attached)

Whole almonds, flaked coconut, chocolate sprinkles, or colored sugar

Melt the chocolates with the fat-free sweetened condensed skimmed milk in a heavy saucepan over low heat or in the microwave. Remove from the heat and stir in the orange rind. Drop by spoonfuls onto a flat surface covered with wax paper or into individual miniature cupcake liners. Decorate with almonds, coconut, chocolate sprinkles, or colored sugar. Put in the freezer or refrigerator to chill until firm. Store covered at room temperature.

Makes 2 dozen pieces

PEACH, PEAR, OR PLUM BRÛLÉE

If your conscience won't let you enjoy a conventional crème brûlée, try this sweet-sour version, which avoids eggs and cream. The sugar caramelizes to give a light crust of brown crunch.

1½ pounds peaches, pears, or plums

½ to ¾ cup packed light brown sugar

1½ cups plain yogurt

½ cup sour cream

Preheat the broiler.

Halve the fruit and remove the pits, seeds, or stones. Place the fruit cut side down in a 9-inch shallow gratin dish. Sprinkle with 2 tablespoons of the sugar. Beat together the yogurt and sour cream. Spread over the fruit and sprinkle with enough of the remaining sugar to coat the top of the fruit. Place under the broiler until the sugar has caramelized, about 5 minutes. Serve hot or cold.

Serves 4

QUICK RICE PUDDING

I got the idea of briefly precooking the rice for rice pudding from my friend Faye Levy's cookbook *30 Low Fat Meals in 30 Minutes.* It certainly speeds up the cooking! I love the new dried fruits, such as cranberries, cherries, and blueberries, as much as I love raisins, candied orange peel, and candied oranges, so I use whatever is at hand.

1 cup short-grain rice, such as Arborio

2 cups milk

1 14-ounce can sweetened condensed milk

1 vanilla bean, split, or 1½ teaspoons vanilla extract

1 tablespoon butter

1 cup dried or candied fruit

2 cups pecans, chopped

Pinch of cinnamon

½ tablespoon grated lemon peel (no white attached)

Bring a large pot of water to the boil. Add the rice, bring back to the boil, and boil 7 minutes. Drain.

Meanwhile, heat the milk, sweetened condensed milk, vanilla bean if using, and butter in a large heavy pot. Add the drained rice, bring to the boil, lower the heat, cover, and simmer 15 minutes. When the rice is tender and the liquid absorbed, remove from the heat. Remove the vanilla bean. Using a fork, stir in the vanilla extract if using, fruit, nuts, cinnamon, and lemon peel.

Serves 4

PEACH FOOL

F ools, like flummeries, are English bits of fluff that worked their way into the American repertoire. Still, for me, they bring to mind long, sunny English summer days, when the evening meal is served while it is still light out. They are perfect for special backyard entertaining, particularly when the grass is green and the flowers are special. Frozen peaches may be used, in which case chilling is sometimes not necessary.

3 ripe peaches
1/4 cup sugar
2/3 cup heavy cream

2 tablespoons chopped pistachios or
  pecans

Peel the peaches and remove the pit. Purée the flesh with the sugar in a food processor or blender until very smooth. Whip the cream, and fold it into the fruit. Spoon into four stemmed glasses or individual containers, cover with plastic wrap, and chill half an hour. Garnish with the nuts before serving.

Serves 4 to 6

BAKED PINEAPPLE ALASKA

Baked Alaska is the *pièce de résistance* of many—if not most—posh cruise dinners. It is ridiculously easy. Pineapple now comes cored and sliced in my grocery store, so I sometimes use some pretty heatproof serving dishes instead of the pineapple shells.

1 very ripe pineapple
2 cups vanilla ice cream, softened
2 tablespoons shredded unsweetened
  coconut

4 egg whites
1/2 cup sugar

Slice the pineapple in half, remove the core, and scoop out the flesh; reserve the shells. Chop fairly finely in a food processor or blender. Pour off any juice and reserve for another purpose. Add the ice cream to the food processor or blender and process until just combined; process in batches if necessary. Spoon the mixture into the reserved pineapple shells, sprinkle with the coconut, and place in the freezer. Whip the egg whites until stiff, fold in the sugar, and beat again to stiff peaks. Spread over the pineapple ice cream and return to the freezer for at least 30 minutes. To serve, preheat the oven to 475°F. Bake the dessert until the meringue browns slightly, about 3 minutes.

Serves 4

CARAMELIZED PEARS AND APPLES

Caramelizing fruit is a wonderful way to snap up the finale to a good meal. Add a little cream when decadence is in order. A good pear to use would be Bosc; a good apple, Granny Smith. This is good by itself, but a fabulous cookie, like a palmier, would make this dessert really stand out.

1 to 2 ripe, firm pears or apples, or a
  combination
1 to 2 tablespoons unsalted butter

1 to 2 tablespoons sugar
½ cup heavy cream (optional)

Slice the unpeeled pear or apple into 6 or 8 wedges, and remove the core and seeds. Melt the butter in a heavy frying pan until hot and singing. Add the fruit wedges and cook on one side for a minute. Sprinkle with sugar and turn. Repeat several times until the fruit is lightly caramelized. Add the cream to the pan and continue to cook until the fruit is soft and the cream has boiled down to half, about 5 minutes. (If the pears or apples are already soft when the cream is added, remove them before preparing the sauce and then pour the warm sauce over when ready to serve.)

Serves 2 to 4

CHOCOLATE-DIPPED FRUIT

A gift of chocolate-dipped fruits from my friend Elizabeth Vaeth reminded me how easy they are to make. I am happy to use dried apricots, pineapples, apples, or pears, but candied oranges and good-quality candied ginger are even nicer. For fresh fruit, use strawberries. The corn syrup gives a bit of gloss, particularly if the fruits are to be refrigerated.

½ cup semisweet chocolate or white
  chocolate bits
2 tablespoons butter

2 tablespoons corn syrup
1½ cups fresh or dried fruit

Melt the chocolate with the butter over low heat or in the microwave. Stir in the corn syrup. Remove from the heat and dip the fruit in the chocolate. Place on a piece of wax paper until set, and then remove to a serving dish. May be refrigerated, taking care to keep the layers separated with wax paper.

Serves 4 to 6

ORANGE FLUMMERY

Flummeries are old-time, fluffy concoctions. They originated in England and came to this country in colonial days. I think of them as mousses and became enamored of them at the London Cordon Bleu. They have a lot of panache for something so easy. The hot syrup should heat the eggs to a minimum of 140° F., which makes them safe to eat.

If you have time to do something a bit more special, hollow out 2 more oranges, freeze the shells, and then roll them in granulated sugar. Pour the Flummery in the shells and refrigerate. (I use an egg carton to stand them up.)

⅓ cup sugar
⅓ cup water
3 eggs, separated

Juice and grated peel (no white attached)
of 3 oranges

Place the sugar and water in a heavy saucepan and heat for a few minutes until the sugar has dissolved. Bring to the boil and boil steadily until thick, about 10 minutes.

Meanwhile beat the egg yolks with an electric mixer until they are thick and light. Continue beating while slowly pouring the hot syrup onto the eggs. Add the juice and peel and beat just until incorporated.

Beat the egg whites until stiff and fold them into the yolk and syrup mixture. Pour into individual stemmed glasses or other containers, cover with plastic wrap, and chill at least 30 minutes or up to several days. As it sits it may separate, and be more like a frothy drink. It's still delicious when you sip it! If the containers are freezerproof, you may place them in the freezer to chill rapidly.

Serves 4 to 6

BEGINNER'S ONE-CRUST PIE DOUGH

Pies seem intimidating to some cooks, but they are actually among the easiest of desserts to make, especially if you've got a prepared crust on hand. What can be easier than rolling, filling, and baking? Double this recipe for a 2-crust pie.

1¼ cups all-purpose flour
½ teaspoon salt

8 tablespoons shortening
3 to 6 tablespoons ice water

Mix the flour and salt together in a bowl. Cut in the shortening with a pastry blender or fork until the mixture resembles cornmeal. Divide the dough into 3 portions. Add some of the ice water, a little at a time, to one portion. Set aside. Repeat with the next portion, adding more water until all the portions are moist. Gather the dough into a smooth ball and flatten into a round. Wrap well with plastic wrap and chill.

Rolling out pie dough: Flour a board, wax paper, or pie cloth. Place the dough round in the center of the floured surface. Starting in the center of the dough, roll to, but not over, the top edge of the dough. Go back to the center, and roll down to, but not over, the bottom edge of the dough. Pick up the dough and turn it a quarter circle. This will keep it round and prevent it from sticking. Repeat your rolling, and repeat the quarter turns until you have a round ⅛ inch thick and 1½ inches larger than your pan. Fold into quarters. Place the pastry in a pie pan with the tip of the triangle in the center and unfold. Trim the pastry 1 inch larger than the pie pan and fold the overhanging pastry under itself. To decorate, press the tines of a fork around the edge, or flute, using two thumbs to pinch the dough all around the edge so that the edge of the dough stands up. Place in the freezer or chill in the refrigerator for 30 minutes before baking if possible.

To prebake: Preheat the oven to 425°F. Crumple a piece of wax paper, then spread it out over the crust to the edges of the pie pan. Fill with raw rice or dried peas. Bake 20 minutes. Carefully remove the paper and rice or peas. (The

PIE CRUST TIME-SAVERS
If it means the difference between making a pie or not making a pie, I see no reason not to use the packaged rounds of ready-made pie dough that are found in the dairy case. They are very handy to keep around and give very creditable results. Another alternative is to make your own dough in quantity, individually wrap flattened disks, and freeze for up to 3 months. Defrost in the refrigerator in the morning and you'll have ready crust by dinnertime.

rice or peas may be used again the next time you prebake a pie crust.) Fill the crust with a filling and bake according to filling directions. If the filling requires no cooking, bake the pie shell 10 minutes more before filling.

Makes dough for 1 crust

BLUEBERRY PIE

We keep searching for a really easy pie and this may be it. Frozen blueberries work far better than the canned. This pie needs to cool completely before cutting to retain its shape. Serve the pie with whipped cream and any leftovers for breakfast the next day.

2 recipes Beginner's One-Crust Pie
  Dough (opposite) or 2 prepared crusts
2 12-ounce bags frozen unsweetened
  blueberries
½ cup sugar

2 tablespoons cornstarch
½ cup sliced almonds
Grated peel (no white attached) of 1
  lemon
1 teaspoon vanilla extract

Preheat the oven to 425°F. Line an 8-inch pie plate with 1 recipe pie dough.

In a large bowl, mix blueberries, sugar, cornstarch, almonds, lemon peel, and vanilla. Stir well to combine. Pour into the unbaked shell. Lightly wet the dough on the rim of the dish. Fold the second dough in quarters and move to the top of the fruit. Unfold the dough to extend to the dampened rim. Press down the two pieces of dough. Decorate, if desired. Cut off excess dough. Cut slits for ventilation and bake until golden brown, 50 to 60 minutes.

Makes 1 pie

RUSTIC APPLE HALF-PIE

This recipe is a great throw-together that somehow seems more exciting than plain apple pie. If you have the time and energy to make your own pie crust, I certainly recommend it. However, I always keep prepared pie crusts around to help out in a pinch.

1 prepared pie crust sheet or 1 recipe
Beginner's One-Crust Pie Dough
(page 196)
3 medium Granny Smith apples,
peeled, cored, and cut into ¼-inch
slices

½ teaspoon cinnamon
½ teaspoon freshly grated nutmeg
2 tablespoons (¼ stick) butter, melted
Pinch of salt
1 tablespoon flour
¼ cup sugar

Preheat the oven to 375°F. Line a baking sheet with aluminum foil and spray with nonstick spray.

Unfold or roll out the pie crust on a floured board to measure 9 inches.

In a large bowl, combine the apple slices, cinnamon, nutmeg, butter, salt, flour, and sugar. Place the apple mixture on half of the pie sheet, leaving a 1-inch border at the edges. Fold the other half of the pastry over the apples, seal the edges with water, and press together with the tines of a fork.

Transfer the half-pie to the prepared baking sheet. Bake 20 to 25 minutes until golden brown. Serve warm or at room temperature.

Makes 1 half-pie

MAPLE YOGURT SAUCE

Quick, simple, and perfect for many desserts, maple-infused yogurt is a lowfat way to enhance apple cobbler, brownies, pies, waffles, pancakes, and crepes. Even easy sauces like this seem like a fancy extra that makes something special really super. This sauce can be made ahead and lasts as long as the original expiration date on the yogurt container.

1 cup plain lowfat yogurt

¼ cup maple syrup

1 teaspoon vanilla extract

In a medium-size bowl, combine the yogurt, syrup, and vanilla and stir until smooth and well blended. Refrigerate until ready to serve.

Makes 1¼ cups

RASPBERRY-LEMON CHEESE PIE

This is an updated version of a classic recipe usually topped with a cherry filling. No one will suspect it's so easy and *so much* lower in fat than the traditional. For real speed, you may use a store-bought crust.

¼ cup unsweetened raspberries, fresh or frozen

1 8-ounce package cream cheese, softened

1 14-ounce can Eagle Brand fat-free sweetened condensed skimmed milk

⅓ cup fresh lemon juice

1 teaspoon vanilla extract

1 8-inch chocolate cookie-crumb crust

Purée the raspberries in a food processor or blender and set aside.

In a large mixer bowl or food processor, beat the cream cheese until fluffy. Gradually beat in the fat-free sweetened condensed skimmed milk until smooth. Stir in the lemon juice and vanilla. Pour into a prepared crust. Drizzle the raspberry purée on top, then swirl through the batter with a knife to create a marbled effect. Refrigerate at least 3 hours before serving.

Serves 6

BIBLIOGRAPHY

Barron, Rosemary. *Flavors of Greece*. New York: William Morrow and Co., Inc., 1991.

Carrier, Robert. *Great Dishes of the World*. London: Thomas Nelson and Sons, Ltd., 1963.

Clayton, Bernard. *Bernard Clayton's New Complete Book of Breads*. New York: Simon and Schuster, 1983.

Cunningham, Marion. *Fannie Farmer Baking Book*. New York: Alfred A. Knopf, 1984.

————. *Fanny Farmer Cookbook*. New York: Alfred A. Knopf, l983.

Cutler, Carol. *Cuisine Rapide*. New York: Clarkson N. Potter, Inc., 1976.

Eckhardt, Linda W., and Diana Butts, *Bread in Half the Time*. New York: Crown Publishers, Inc., 1991.

Fisher, Leah Loeb, and Maria Robbins. *Mama Leah's Jewish Kitchen*. New York: Macmillan, 1990.

Foster, Carol. *Short Cuts to Great Cuisine*. Freedom, Calif.: The Crossing Press, 1994.

Franey, Pierre, and Bryan Miller. *Cuisine Rapide*. New York: Times Books, 1989.

Gates, Laura, and Ann Binney. *Brownies, Blondies and Bar Cookies*. Tucson: HP Books, 1991.

Goldbeck, Nikki, and David Goldbeck. *American Whole Foods Cuisine*. New York: New American Library, 1983.

Greene, Bert. *Greene on Greens*. New York: Workman Publishing, 1984.

Hazan, Giuliano. *The Classic Pasta Cookbook*. New York: Dorling Kindersley, 1993.

Hazelton, Nika. *The Regional Italian Kitchen*. New York: M. Evans and Co., Inc., 1978.

Jolly, Martine. *Le Chocolat*. New York: Random House, 1985.

Junior League of Savannah. *Savannah Style*. Savannah: 1980.

Kamman, Madeleine. *In Madeleine's Kitchen*. New York: Atheneum, 1984.

Leahy, Linda Romanelli, with Jack Maguire. *World's Greatest Peanut Butter Cookbook.* New York: Villard Books, 1994.

Lemlin, Jeanne. *Vegetarian Pleasures.* New York: Alfred A. Knopf, 1986.

Mondodori, Arnoldo, ed. *Feast of Italy.*: New York: Thomas Y. Crowell Co., 1973.

Netzer, Corrine T. *101 Low Calorie Recipes.* New York: Dell Publishing, 1993.

Rombauer, Irma S., and Marion Rombauer Becker. *Joy of Cooking,* New York: New American Library, Inc., 1964.

Schafer, Charles, and Violet Schafer. *Wokcraft.* San Francisco: Verba Buena Press, 1942.

Schloss, Andrew, with Ken Bookman. *Fifty Ways to Cook Most Everything.* New York: Simon and Schuster, 1992.

INDEX

EQUIVALENT IMPERIAL AND METRIC MEASUREMENTS

American cooks use standard containers, the 8-ounce cup and a tablespoon that takes exactly 16 level fillings to fill that cup level. Measuring by cup makes it very difficult to give weight equivalents, as a cup of densely packed butter will weigh considerably more than a cup of flour. The easiest way therefore to deal with cup measurements in recipes is to take the amount by volume rather than by weight. Thus the equation reads:

1 cup = 240 ml = 8 fl. oz.   ½ cup = 120 ml = 4 fl. oz.

It is possible to buy a set of American cup measures in major stores around the world.

In the States, butter is often measured in sticks. One stick is the equivalent of 8 tablespoons. One tablespoon of butter is therefore the equivalent to 1⁄2 ounce/15 grams.

Liquid Measures

Fluid ounces	U.S.	Imperial	Milliliters
	1 teaspoon	1 teaspoon	5
¼	2 teaspoon	1 dessert spoon	7
½	1 tablespoon	1 tablespoon	15
1	2 tablespoon	2 tablespoon	28
2	¼ cup	4 tablespoon	56
4	½ cup or ¼ pint		110
5		¼ pint or 1 gill	140
6	¾ cup		170
8	1 cup or ½ pint		225
9			250, ¼ liter
10	1¼ cups	½ pint	280
12	1½ cups	¾ pint	340
15	¾ pint		420
16	2 cups or 1 pint		450
18	2¼ cups		500, ½ liter
20	2½ cups	1 pint	560
24	3 cups		675
			or 1½ pints
25		1¼ pints	700
27	3½ cups		750
30	33⁄4 cups	1½ pints	840
32	4 cups or 2 pints		900
	or 1 quart		
35		1¾ pints	980
36	4½ cups		1000, 1 liter
40	5 cups	2 pints or 1 quart	1120
	or 2½ pints		
48	6 cups or 3 pints		1350
50		2½ pints	1400
60	7½ cups	3 pints	1680
64	8 cups or 4 pints		1800
	or 2 quarts		
72	9 cups		2000, 2 liters

Solid Measures

U.S. and Imperial Measures		Metric Measures	
ounces	pounds	grams	kilos
1		28	
2		56	
3 ½		100	
4	¼	112	
5		140	
6		168	
8	½	225	
9		250	¼
12	¾	340	
16	1	450	
18		500	½
20	1¼	560	
24	1½	675	
27		750	3⁄4
28	1¾	780	
32	2	900	
36	2¼	1000	1
40	2½	1100	
48	3	1350	
54		1500	1½
64	4	1800	
72	4½	2000	2
80	5	2250	2¼
90		2500	2½
100	6	2800	2¾

Oven Temperature Equivalents

Fahrenheit	Celsius	Gas Mark	Description
225	110	¼	Cool
250	130	½	
275	140	1	Very Slow
300	150	2	
325	170	3	Slow
350	180	4	Moderate
375	190	5	
400	200	6	Moderately Hot
425	220	7	Fairly Hot
450	230	8	Hot
475	240	9	Very Hot
500	250	10	Extremely Hot

Linear and Area Measures

1 inch	2.54 centimeters
1 foot	0.3048 meters
1 square inch	6.4516 square centimeters
1 square foot	929.03 square centimeters